Dear Tina,

Congratulations on your latest transformation!

The Book On
TRANSFORMATION

WITH BERNADETTE RIDGE

Continued blessings,

B Ridge

JAN FRASER INSPIRED LIFE SERIES

The Book On

TRANSFORMATION

WITH BERNADETTE RIDGE

Foreword by Jack Canfield, co-creator of Chicken Soup for the Soul® and co-author of The Success Principles™

First Edition

Copyright ©2022 Jan Fraser Inspired Life Series
www.janfraser.com

ISBN: 978-1-7378728-7-0

Acknowledgements
Director of Book Production: Jennie Ritchie | www.jennieritchie.com
Book Designer: Sue Luehring | sjldesign.carbonmade.com
Website designer: Myrto Mangrioti | www.loving-living.com

www.thebookontransformation.com

We dedicate this book to you . . . our sisters, friends, mothers, aunts, grandmothers, teachers, and leaders who inspire the world daily. In this, we honor the many women who have gone before us, lighting our path and teaching us the quality of Courageous Transformation.

No matter your circumstance, your country, your story, we walk alongside each of you in the search for more successful transformations in your life and in the world.

To Your Success in Transformation . . .

CONTRIBUTING AUTHORS

Regina Andler – *USA*
Barbara Blue – *Ireland*
Paddy Briggs – *Canada*
Victoria Chadderton – *USA*
Ilka V. Chavez – *Panama*
Sophia Chow – *China*
Karen Durham – *Bermuda*
Alynn Godfroy – *Canada*
Jackie Graybill – *USA*
Robin Eldridge Hain – *USA*
LouAnne Hunt – *Canada*
Sally Huss – *USA*
Linda Rose Jensen – *USA*
Addy Kujawa – *USA*
Lila Larson – *Canada*
Artemis-Pallas Liontas – *Greece*

Marjorie Lombard – *USA*
Sue London – *Canada*
Michele Lutz – *USA*
Myrto Mangrioti – *Greece*
Sarah McCalden – *England*
Janis Neary Miller – *USA*
Echo Laymon Pelster – *USA*
Laarni Cordova Reyes –
The Philippines
Bernadette Ridge – *USA*
Jennie Ritchie – *USA*
Cherylanne Thomas – *USA*
Lorraine Thomson – *Canada*
KDB (Karmen De Bora)
Wheeler – *USA*
Jane Williams – *USA*

Reprinted with Permissions

TABLE OF CONTENTS

Treasured Transformations

Triumphant Transformations

Invitation

INTRODUCTION

Welcome to our Inspired Life Community and The Book on Transformation®

As we view the world today, we see change happening all around us. It is in the air. Much of this change is inspiring.

If you want to change the world, help the women.
— Nelson Mandela

The Book on Transformation® was born out of necessity to help, bolster and support women on their journeys and life paths to greater growth and living their highest potential.

Women around the globe are finding the strength to create transformation in their lives. Whether that means starting a business from scratch, gaining the confidence to leave an abusive relationship, navigating health challenges or a host of other circumstances, life is changing.

I have undergone countless transformations in my own life.

In my career, I have worked chairside and managed an orthodontic office, retail sales, insurance adjuster, baggage handler, flight attendant and professional trainer and speaker.

In my relationships, I have been married more times than the average person and worked through the ups and downs of living and loving. I have spoken in nearly every state in the USA and traveled to six of the seven continents of the world.

One thing I know . . . though the process of transformation is often risky and uncertain as to the journey or result, it is continually about learning and growth.

Both are necessary for us to flourish in life.

That is the purpose of this book. To help you create transformation in your life. It doesn't matter if the change is something you chose or it was chosen for you. It doesn't matter if the shift seems like a small thing to other people and not to you.

The power to transform is within you. It's within me. It's within all of us.

The book is designed in five sections, all touching on types of Transformations: Thoughtful, Timely, Together, Treasured and Triumphant. The stories and content of all the 30 courageous women authors are original and vulnerable. When they share their journeys of transformation in their own words, you will feel that you are walking each step with them. Their purpose is to inspire you to move forward in your own transformation with confidence and clarity

The Book on Transformation® is the second volume in the Inspired Life Series. In each of the forthcoming books, we will assist, support and suggest ways that you could live a more inspired life. This is only the beginning . . .

Transformation is a life-enhancing process to be discovered, embraced and shared. Some find an essential oil used daily gives them strength and inspiration on their journey. If you would like to experience the essential oil called "Transformation" and find out for yourself if this could help and spur you on, reach out to me at info@janfraser.com and our team will send you a free sample.

With this book as your inspiration, may we all seek to become our best selves and live life on our own terms.

Here's to your successful transformations!

Loving Hugs,

Jan

Jack Canfield

Jack Canfield, known as America's #1 Success Coach, is a best-selling author, professional speaker, trainer, and entrepreneur. He is the founder and CEO of the Canfield Training Group, which trains entrepreneurs, educators, corporate leaders and motivated individuals how to accelerate the achievement of their personal and professional goals.

He has conducted live trainings for more than a million people in more than 50 countries around the world. He holds two Guinness World Record titles and is a member of the National Speakers Association's Speaker Hall of Fame.

Jack is the coauthor of more than two hundred books, including, T*he Success Principles™: How to Get from Where You Are to Where You Want to Be, The Success Principles Workbook,* and the *Chicken Soup for the Soul®* series, which includes forty New York Times bestsellers and has sold more than 500 million copies in 47 languages around the world.

Jack is a featured teacher in the movie *The Secret,* and has appeared on more than a thousand radio and television shows, including *The Oprah Winfrey Show, Oprah's Super Soul Sunday, the Today show, Fox & Friends,* and *Larry King Live.*

Foreword

By Jack Canfield

Co-Creator of the best-selling *Chicken Soup for the Soul®* series
Co-Author of *The Success Principles*™

The dictionary defines transformation as a "change in form, appearance, nature, or character." The stories in this book are stories of transformation, in some cases radical changes of perspective, paradigms, beliefs, self-confidence, self-expression, and self-actualization – often resulting in a strong commitment to help others transform as well.

The women in this book share how their transformational experiences changed how they see the world, how they see themselves, how they see their ability to accomplish their dreams, and how they can help others believe that they, too, can accomplish their dreams.

My professional life has been dedicated to facilitating the same kinds of transformation that these authors write about. My professional life began in Chicago as a teacher of inner-city high school students, most of whom did not believe that they had the ability to accomplish their goals and heartfelt dreams. Their beliefs about what was possible were in definite need of transformation. After I became aware of this, I quickly became as interested in how to facilitate that transformation as I was in teaching history and social studies. In order to help my students, I began to take workshops on achievement motivation, building high self-esteem and the principles of success.

When I integrated what I was learning into my curriculum, I watched my students come alive. They began to believe in themselves and their dreams. I was gratified that many of them went on to attend college and create successful careers.

As my career unfolded, I went on to teach these same principles and practices to thousands of other teachers and also wrote several best-selling books on the topic. Later, I started my own training company devoted solely to teaching the principles and practices of transformation and breakthrough success through trainings, speaking, online courses, and books, including the *Chicken Soup for the Soul®* series and *The Success Principles™* books. Presently, I also train transformational trainers through our Train the Trainer Programs.

My current goal is to have One Million Transformational Trainers teaching our Breakthrough to Success principles around the world. We have only recently taken on this goal, but there are already more than 3500 certified trainers living and teaching in 117 countries around the world.

So, what does all of this have to do with *The Book on Transformation*, which you now hold in your hands? Well, the thirty heart-centered authors of this book, who also come from all around the world, are all graduates of my Breakthrough to Success and Train the Trainer programs. And through their commitment to working on developing themselves and becoming all they can be, they have all come to know that intentionally pursuing and sometimes simply surrendering to the process of transformation is a key ingredient to fulfilling their life purpose and finding true happiness and fulfillment in their lives.

These thirty women are speakers, trainers, coaches, teachers, counselors, and mentors who have had to deal with many challenges. They could have given up and succumbed to those challenges, but instead, they chose to face them head on with grit and determination, and thereby transform both their experiences and themselves. And now they are committed to share their hard-earned wisdom to inspire, encourage and empower you to do the same.

Having co-authored more than 200 *Chicken Soup for the Soul®* books, which are read in more than fifty languages all over the world, bringing hope, courage, inspiration and love to millions of people, I know how these types of stories of resiliency and triumph over adversity are an unquestionably powerful tool to support transformation in your life and the lives of those you love. So, I encourage you to read all the stories and allow them to deeply touch you and transform you.

As you'll soon discover, The Book on Transformation is a treasure chest full of transformational tools for you to take advantage of – whether you are a woman who may have given up on achieving your dreams and goals, or if you are simply someone who would like some extra encouragement in realizing your life purpose.

No matter how small or large your current challenges are or have been, reading this book will help you to find the courage to commit to embarking upon or continuing your own transformational journey.

Finally, I'd like to share a way that you can further enhance your experience of reading this book. I encourage you to get a hold of a bottle of the Young Living essential oil blend called "Transformation" and diffuse it if you have a diffuser, or simply drop several drops into the palm of your non-dominant hand, then rub tour hands together and inhale the aroma for 20 seconds or more before you start reading. You'll discover that this magical blend of essential oils will actually activate and facilitate your own opening to the experience of transformation. I've been using it along with many other Young Living oils for the last three years, and they have been a powerful facilitator of my own and my students' transformation. Jan Fraser, who compiled this book, as well as many of the authors in this book have also been successfully using these oils for themselves and with their clients. You can contact Jan at www.janfraser.com for more information on the oils.

My wish for you is that you will read all of these stories, be inspired by and apply what you learn, and achieve all your heartfelt dreams.

Love to you!

Jack Canfield

Jan Fraser

Jan is a 'self-starter', bringing real world customer service experience to her keynotes, training and coaching. An airline industry superstar, she rose from the ramp support team to instructor, training thousands of flight attendants.

Jan was a Seminar Speaker for Skill Path and National Seminars, and Adjunct Professor at Bermuda College. She is a Success and Writing Coach and traveled the world to deliver training in the US and seven countries.

Jan is a sought after Keynote Speaker. She is the author of nine books and coaches writers through virtual and onsite retreats. She co-created the *Success University for Women* series and is the Creator of the Jan Fraser Inspired Life Series best sellers.

She has a CSP® (Certified Speaking Professional™) designation from the National Speakers Association.

Jan lives with her husband in Lake Las Vegas and Bermuda, balancing her life between two shores.

Contact

Website: www.janfraser.com
Email: jan@janfraser.com

Live Your Inspired Life

By Jan Fraser

"Decide . . . whether or not the goal is worth the risks involved. If it is, stop worrying . . ."

— Amelia Earhart, America's Famous Aviatrix

What was I thinking? I promised a girlfriend I would jump out of a plane with her. Had I lost my mind? It was a perfectly good, though tiny, aircraft. Yes, as a flight attendant, I was used to being onboard an aircraft at 37,000 feet . . . I never thought I'd be jumping out of one!

I was in my mid-fifties, and I had decided, now, or never. When the invitation was extended, I thought better to do it when I still have the energy and the desire to go for it. My girlfriend was half my age and a registered nurse. She said, "If anything happens to you, I'll fix you up when we get on the ground."

We decided to do the highest freefall dive you could do without oxygen, 14,000 feet. It seemed doable, but I started to get nervous when I signed the papers releasing them from all liability if I somehow landed wrong or didn't survive the jump.

When I fit into the skinny 'zip-up' jumpsuit, I was feeling svelte. In the 45-minute orientation, we watched a movie where you pretend to be a flying banana. The jump was over Lake Mead in Nevada, and I'm a swimmer. I decided, 'Okay, no problem. If I land in the lake instead of on the ground, I'll just swim my way to the shore.' Of course, these are all the things you say to yourself to make it easier to take the leap.

We wore leather helmets and goggles that looked like Bullwinkle. It would have been comical, if I wasn't so scared. We climbed aboard the plane, the size of a flying tent trailer and sat in fear on the floor.

Going to 14,000 feet for our jump took a long time. It was like a root canal that wouldn't stop. We kept flying and flying and I'm thinking, 'Why did I agree to this?'

I was constantly repeating the mantra that I learned in experiential training with American Airlines. 'Stop, Challenge and Choose.' Stop yourself from letting your mind roll on. Challenge yourself to go through with whatever your goal is. Choose to make the decision to take that step toward transformation.

When the pilot said I was going out first, I was startled. He leaned across the cockpit and threw the door open. My tandem instructor shouted at me over the wind, telling me to work my way to the door. Now, we were clipped together by our harnesses and pigeon-walked together to the door opening.

He said to me, "I need you to get your right foot on the wing, outside the plane."

I asked. "How am I going to do that?" It was a long way out there. I made a couple of attempts with no luck until my third lunge for the wing. There was so much open-air space.

I didn't want to look down.

I reached farther and got my foot toward the wing and then we started to roll and tumble out of the aircraft. We were flying! He pulled the the rip cord, and we started to drift more gently because the parachute had unfurled.

The feeling of flying as we were drifting and floating to the ground was incredible. I was on top of the world. I even held the parachute ropes for a time guiding us safely to the ground.

When I landed, standing with my toes 'up' because I didn't want to stove them into the ground . . . I was giddy. I made it. I survived and I was a new person as a result of the jump.

When I jumped out of that plane, my molecular structure changed. I transformed.

Since that jump, if I needed to do something difficult, whether it be physical, emotional, or intellectual, I have discovered greater strength and confidence to achieve it. This applies to anything that we do while in a transformation. When you stretch yourself beyond what you thought you could do, you are changed deep inside, different and braver and more courageous as a result.

Celebrate every time you took a leap in your life. Whether that's out of an aircraft door, stepping on stage, speaking up at work, or helping your family . . . You did it.

That's transformation.

It requires strength and courage, taking risks, and exhibiting fortitude. We don't always know what any transformation will require of us. We don't know what lies ahead...it could be an endless blue ocean . . . it could feel like we're flying solo. Yet, we have the power within us to create and transform our life. If we go forward, we can create a different life, a better life.

One of the women in history who exemplified this steely determination to create better lives for women was the heroic Amelia Earhart. She wanted "To create a life without fear and encouraged women to have a can-do attitude." I've always felt a connection to Amelia because she was part of my dad's life story.

My Father Met Amelia Earhart

While talking with my father about his early service days in the Army Air Corps, precursor to the United States Air Force, he shared an amazing story with me.

While in the South Pacific Islands working as a Crew Chief, he met Amelia Mary Earhart, the famous aviatrix. He and his crew repaired her damaged plane and assured her safety on her flight back to the United States.

The next flight around the globe was her last as we know she was headed to Howland Island and disappeared from radar and the World.

She wrote a message only days before that flight:

"Not much more than a month ago, I was on the
other shore of the Pacific, looking westward. This
evening, I looked eastward over the Pacific. In those
fast-moving days, which have intervened, the
whole width of the world has passed behind us,
except this broad ocean. I shall be glad
when we have the hazards of its navigation behind us."
— Amelia Earhart

Amelia was born 50 years before me in Atchinson, Kansas, a 12 hour drive from my birthplace of Canton, Ohio. Now, commercial air travel would take hardly longer than a nap onboard to arrive in her birth city from mine on a sleek jet.

When she was 10, she had her first plane ride, and was hooked into her dream from then on. In 1932, at the age of 35, she became a pioneer in the field of aviation, as the first woman to complete a solo, nonstop transatlantic flight. This was at a time when women were home baking apple pie and taking care of the homestead, while most accomplishments were completed and awarded to men.

She had courage, strength, and fortitude to do what she did as a woman, regardless of judgment from the public in those early days. In doing what no women had ever done before, she set the bar and raised expectations for women.

"What was Amelia like?" I asked my Dad. He thought about it and replied, "She was good-looking and tall for a woman of that time and had a radiant smile. She was friendly and kind speaking to me and all the crew though she was the heroine. She thanked us continually for helping her and mending her plane. She left an indelible impression on me and the entire crew as a miraculous, yet humble person."

Amelia changed people's vision of what women could do. She accomplished a lifetime in her 40 years of life.

She inspired women, including me, to get outside our 'comfort zones' and make a change which is what happened on a wilderness experience I had some years ago.

Amelia Inspired Me

It was one of the scariest decisions of my life . . . Taking a wilderness experience from the University of Santa Barbara, that involved travel to Northern California, high Sierra Mountains and to live five days in the wilderness.

Two of those days would be completely solo, no humans, no voices.

I wasn't a mountaineering woman. I did like to put on boots and go hiking a bit, but nothing like what I experienced in the Sierras. I was 'light years' from my 'comfort zone!'

I wanted to impress my then dating partner and spend more time with him as he was a survivalist. I lied when I told him, "I can do that wilderness trip with you, nothing frightens me. I'm a big girl."

We were a part of a larger group, hiking up the mountains with our food, clothing and supplies in our backpacks. My body was hurting as my backpack bounced heavily on my hip bones. I was putting on a brave face though the pain was increasing. I knew I was in too deep to 'chicken-out' now.

The solo experience began the day after our arrival at the group campsite.

We were all placed in separate areas a mile apart from each other. I was all alone in a personal campsite with the wildlife and my water source. The instructions were to place a rock a certain direction before the sun was straight overhead (approximately 12 noon). The next person one mile away would come to the rock location to see if it had been moved. If the rock had been moved, they would know I was still alive.

My only way to get water was to walk down to a creek area that was known to be infested with California rattlesnakes. They said, "The way to identify the snakes is to go down the first time to the creek and memorize where the twigs and branches are overlaying on the path. Then, the next time you go down the same path, if you notice a branch moved, it was a snake."

I was extremely careful where I stepped on the path and while I leaned over the creek to fill my canteen.

At night, I was in my portable pup tent that had an opening on both ends. I could hear the wild pigs, the javelinas, snorting, and running through my little campsite. I scrunched down in my sleeping bag for fear they would run through my tent and crush me. I did not sleep well.

I made my campsite as cozy as I could. I kept to a schedule of cleaning the area, writing in my journal, cooking meals and filling my canteen with water.

After two days and nights of never hearing a sound from a human being, I was ready to return to our group campsite. It was shocking to me how much I missed human interaction.

While I was in my solo, one EMT hiker was bitten by a rattlesnake and our guide suffered a concussion. There was danger in the wilderness and, through it all, I had transformed from a mildly fit hiker to a wilderness woman.

I felt like a pioneer, like Amelia Earhart.

Like her, I was flying solo for 48 hours. I can imagine that when she was alone in her cockpit she must have summoned her courage and strength.

I felt close to Amelia when I jumped out of the plane and sustained myself in the Sierras. Sometimes, we are flying solo in our transformations.

You're in the right place to navigate yours.

In the hopes they will help you, I want to share some STANDUP Transformation Tips that I've learned from my experiences:

Support . . . Let someone know what you're doing and where you're going. Know how to contact others.

Time . . . Is this the best time to invest in this transformation?

Awareness . . . It could save your life or make life easier.

New and Noteworthy . . . Celebrate this new transforming venture and journal your progress.

Danger and Pitfalls . . . What could go wrong and steps to prevent its happening.

Understand . . . Interview others who may have taken that path before. Learn.

Plan, Pack with Purpose . . . Plan with a purpose. Pack resources like food, water, information and equipment.

"I want to do it because I want to do it.
Women must try to do things as men
have tried when they fail their failure
must be but a challenge to others."
—Amelia Earhart

You're in the right place. We believe in you. You have us on your Transformation Team. You are not flying solo.

Go for it!

Go and Live Your Inspired Life!

Bernadette Ridge

B ernadette is originally from Ireland and now lives on Spinnaker Island, close to Boston, MA. She is a former teacher with a B. Ed. Degree, and a seasoned Workforce Engagement enterprise solutions sales specialist. She has achieved certifications in Strategic Intervention coaching, Miracle-Minded Coaching, Barrett Values System Leadership & Coaching, Jack Canfield/Kathleen Seeley Virtual Skills Trainer in The Success Principles, Applied Positive Psychology and Infinite Possibilities, amongst others.

As a former President of a Boston organization committed to promoting the Irish language, she was included in a history book about people who made a difference between Connemara and Boston over the past 30 years. She is a member of the Healy World and Young Living organization. Bernadette has a huge desire to create a legacy by making our world more joyful. She is training for a TEDx talk and is creating a coaching business around 'TrailBlazing from Trauma to Joy'. For more information SOON, visit her website.

Contact
Website: www.BernadetteRidge.com
Email: bernadette.ridge@gmail.com

The Joyful Journey of Transformation

By Bernadette Ridge

"There is an unseen life that dreams us; it knows our true direction and destiny. We can trust ourselves more than we realize, and we need have no fear of change."

—John O'Donohue

I remember waking up this past Christmas on December 28, 2021 in my childhood bed actually feeling **grateful** that I got the dreaded Covid. My symptoms were mild, thankfully, and so were my 86-year-old dad's. It caused major inconvenience with return travel plans to Boston, being confined to home and unable to co-mingle with family that I had not physically seen in over two years. However, I was pleasantly aware of my thoughts, feelings, reactions and behaviors.

For years now, I have been deliberately fine tuning my point of attraction – what I focus on. I could feel that things were changing for me, and it occurred to me that what was actually happening was not that I was in "new places," but that I was changing and becoming "new" in those same places. I was in my family home in Connemara, on Ireland's western coast. I was seeing every family member, every place, every thing as a new experience, and that brought me joy and fresh energy with each day.

The world as we have known it seems to be discombobulating before our eyes and, understandably, people are freaking out. It can feel apocalyptic, where an old way of doing things meets a new way, when who we were gives way to who we are becoming, and the world as we have known it before is shattered, so a new world can take it's place. Psychically, this can feel disconcerting as the new you is not always embraced or given welcome by the old you. And yet, the new you will prevail because nature favors the forward movement of life. For some people, a cancer diagnosis, death of a spouse, an unexpected divorce, getting sober or major life changing events can be at the heart of transformation, and though hard won, is a new found peace.

Recognizing that there was as much we learned from our past failures as from our successes, from our pain as from our joys, and from our trials as from our good times, we saw that everything we had been through had prepared us for this time. This is why I love John O'Donohue's quote so much. It also explains our yearning to become who we are meant to be, and general dissatisfaction with our lives if we are not. So, to his point, this is not a time to be frightened but recognize how deeply informed we are, and that we are more prepared than we seem to think we are for giving birth to what needs to happen now.

At a macro level, going through a global pandemic, wars in other countries, and atrocities on our own doorsteps, has given us a taste for peace. Our knowing what was at stake in our own lives now makes us more capable of creating peace on a larger scale. We should honor ourselves for having survived what we have been through and recognize it as a form of transformation.

We feel the hope of something incredible being born out of what has transpired.

On a personal level, it was a shock to finally leave home to return to Boston, and then hear of the deaths of my uncle, first, and within days of his burial, my beloved father's passing. Uncle Mairtin had cancer which had, sadly, recurred, and this time, his endurance was mercifully brief and he was buried on the occasion of my dad's 87th birthday. Four days later, my dad died peacefully in his sleep.

My uncle was celebrated for his work, much of which was 'dark', culminating in a book called *Breaking the Silence – One Garda's (policeman) Quest to Find the Truth*, published in April 2008. Uncle Mairtin had sent me a Christmas card which I received in mid-January, on my return to Boston. It touched my soul on many levels, and his last sentence in the card reads: "You bring light to our soul," signing off with "Yours, in kindness and love."

I will treasure this card forever, for it speaks to his own transformation and mine.

The other card that touches my heart, makes me laugh and cry. It is my dad's last birthday card to me. It reads "Happy birthday to a rare bird!" Inside the card he wrote a few things, all in Irish/Gaelic, but the gist of it is this: "I wanted to get something special for your birthday but I don't think they will allow you to bring 'rooster' potatoes with you to Boston, without consequences. I was thinking of you going to the hairdresser to change your style, on your birthday, before returning to Boston, and I thought you might come home to me with a pink hair-do, like your aunt. But, much like I thought about you occasionally before, I was wrong! Thank you, from my heart, for your cooking and your company. Love and ever more respect forever, your Dad. Xoxo."

Loss and grief also cause transformation. I am now an orphan. I am deeply grateful for the extended, quality time I had with my dad at Christmas and into January. That seems like a blessing now, in hindsight. Listening to my dad's two-part eulogy, delivered magnificently by my uncle and brother, filled me with pride and fresh determination to live my life as well as he did, using my God-given talents to benefit the world.

Darkness is natural and not something to be feared, though it does lead people into sorrow, disappointment and anger. By choosing to be a positive force in the world, our vibration drives out the dark and ushers in hope, love and joy. We all have the spiritual depth and wisdom to be able to make a great difference in a world which needs our unique gifts and talents now more than ever.

For myself, I know that my purpose is to bring light and joy to the world. Yes, the decisions to leave countries twice, careers twice, marriages twice were transformational in their own right. But, I think what my family perceived and acknowledged this Christmas and during our father's funeral, not having physically seen each other for two long years and with the gift of almost a month together, was deeper than the adaptability required to "move on" or say yes to opportunities of a lifetime, as I thankfully did. I had notably changed.

My sisters talked to me about experiencing me as "calm", more "myself" than they had ever recollected. My youngest sister even used the term "golden" to describe my demeanour, which warmed my heart. Although it was a little surprising to hear the conversation out loud, it was also deeply reassuring, as I had been sensing for some time that I had reached a new place within.

As I had a lot of alone time to reflect, it occurred to me that I had not felt anxious or hurt or any negative emotions in a long time, even in the light of some challenging situations. The realization was almost momentarily transformative in its own right! I had been following a lot of Marianne Williamson and Mike Dooley's work around the spiritual dimensions of transformation, the power of God, the Universe and the integrated connectedness of everything. I wish I could explain it better but it's really not an intellectual concept; it's more of a deep-rooted feeling or belief system. Perhaps it's more important for me to try to share what it actually feels like, so you are encouraged to find your own path to a similar state.

First, it is deeply liberating in the sense that I totally understand the power of thoughts over feelings and actions. Having control over your thoughts means you can look at any given situation differently. A Course in Miracles says a miracle is simply a shift in perception.

Second, that deep awareness is energizing! Even with Covid symptoms, I wanted to push through my fatigue because I felt like cooking a nice dinner for my dad and me, and everyone knows I am not a cook! I also wanted to go for a long walk whenever the Irish weather was conducive – and I did.

Third, adopting this awareness created a deep inner sense of peace and tranquility that is unshakable.

The opportunity to participate in this collaborative Book on Transformation is part of my new journey. Ours truly are lives with infinite possibilities, if we can just get out of our own way and let it be. As

Nanette Matthews says, "*Just remember life is your creation and you can dismantle it and re-create it.*"

I will end my chapter with a gift to you. It is a poem that, for me, describes the joyful journey of magnificent personal transformation. It is from John O'Donohue's *To Bless the Space Between Us.*

FOR A NEW BEGINNING

In out-of-the-way places of the heart,
Where your thoughts never think to wander,
This beginning has been quietly forming,
Waiting until you were ready to emerge.
For a long time it has watched your desire,
Feeling the emptiness growing inside you,
Noticing how you willed yourself on,
Still unable to leave what you had outgrown.
It watched you play with the seduction of safety
And the gray promises that sameness whispered,
Heard the waves of turmoil rise and relent,
Wondered would you always live like this.
Then the delight, when your courage kindled,
And out you stepped onto new ground,
Your eyes young again with energy and dream,
A path of plenitude opening before you.
Though your destination is not yet clear
You can trust the promise of this opening;
Unfurl yourself into the grace of beginning
That is at one with your life's desire.
Awaken your spirit to adventure;
Hold nothing back, learn to find ease in risk;
Soon you will be home in a new rhythm,
For your soul senses the world that awaits you.

JAN FRASER INSPIRED LIFE SERIES

Thoughtful
TRANSFORMATIONS

Laarni Cordova Reyes

L aarni Cordova Reyes is a charming, gracious professional from The Philippines which is an archipelago comprising more than 7,100 islands covering nearly 300,000 square kilometers which is 186,000 miles.

She was born in the Municipality of Orani in the Province of Bataan in a family with three daughters. Her strength and focus are unrivaled as she sold her car to enroll in International Academy for Aesthetic Sciences.

Laarni took a bus three hours one way to Manilla to achieve her Certification as a PhilbeautiQ Internationally Accredited Master PhilbeautiQ Instructor/Technician. She creates natural looking eyebrows, eyelier and lip liner to the delight of her clients.

In her free time, she enjoys zooming with her family, cooking and the culinary arts, essential oils, and driving.

Laarni has an adult son and daughter who are in college currently. She lives with her husband in Bermuda bringing beauty to the women of the island while enjoying her dream job.

I Sold My Car

By Laarni Cordova Reyes

"The road to success comes through hard work, determination and sacrifice."

— Anonymous

Yes, I sold my car. I could always take the bus, though it was long and tiring at times. My car could not give me what I wanted, my lifelong dream.

It could not give me my transformation.

However, when I sold it, the money I received set me on the path to my amazing transformation.

Looking back, long before I drove a car, I always wanted to be a make-up artist. Growing up in the Philippines with extended family, I borrowed my nephews when I was 10 years old to apply make-up and practice on them.

They were fun and flexible and allowed me to put make-up on their knees and I practiced long afternoons on them. It was a distant dream to become a make-up artist and make women feel more beautiful.

I originally wanted to be an elementary school teacher and was in training to do that when I got the news. I was pregnant and needed to quit school and raise my baby so teaching would have to come later in life.

With my children almost grown, in the 11th grade in school and my husband, I remembered my childhood dream of becoming a make-up artist. I researched the training schools near my home, but, I did not have the money to make it happen. Then, I realized, I had a car which I could sell and pay for my Cosmetology Training.

I didn't question this reasoning. I just did it. I took the leap and figured the opportunity was now and I needed to make it happen.

I paid for my training with the money from selling my car. We were for a time, without a car and yet, I felt so good because I was moving in life toward my childhood dream.

Studying hard, working through challenges, and in the passage of time, I graduated as a Certified International Make-up Artist with a semi-permanent make-up technology degree! Hallelujah!

Once I started my business, I found clients close by and from other islands. They would come to me to make them beautiful. My dream was coming true. Women flew into a nearby airport to have me work with them. It completely surprised me that they would do that.

I enjoyed all my experiences. I was interviewed and asked why or how I became so successful at my work.

I responded, "I love what I do. I don't worry about competition. I work well and I make my customers feel comfortable while I am working on them. I have a light hand and they don't feel any pressure or pain."

I had arrived at this success, and it felt good.

Recently, another opportunity for transformation was on its way to me. My husband started working on the island of Bermuda and after a few years, I was able to secure a job in a top salon there, too.

Because I transformed myself from a housewife to a professional cosmetologist, I used the same courage and risk-taking to move my business and skills to Bermuda from the Philippines. I am starting a new passage of my life with my husband and all the clients who will come to me for my light hands and kindness.

Transformation is what has given me the ability to acknowledge that my moving forward, having patience in the process and faith in the outcome works well for me. This life change is a huge joyful win for me and my family.

Selling my car was the best thing that I could have ever done.

Linda Rose Jensen

Linda Jensen has been licensed in the financial services industry since 1994 and is committed to maintaining the highest standards of integrity and professionalism. Linda is a Certified Financial Educator and a SOFA Financial Literacy Instructor. She has conducted regular seminars for the public and business professionals on a variety of topics for the past 24 years. She specializes in retirement and income planning as well as tax planning, long term care planning and estate planning. Linda is a holistic fiduciary financial planner who always has her client's best interests at heart. She is passionate about helping her clients create a successful retirement with an emphasis of avoiding the many risks of retirement.

Linda and her husband Brad met in college. They enjoy the Pacific Northwest and are proud to call it home. They love spending time with their children and grandchildren. Linda is a life-long learner who enjoys reading, hiking, cooking and sewing.

Contact
Website: www.heartfinancialgroup.com

A Richer and Deeper Life

By Linda Rose Jensen

"The pearls weren't really white, they were a warm oyster beige, with little knots in between so if they broke, you only lost one. I wished my life could be like that, knotted up so that even if something broke, the whole thing wouldn't come apart."

— Janet Fitch

Sometimes patterns happen that get your attention. Sometimes fear happens to change your direction. Sometimes a breakthrough happens so dramatic that we are compelled to make a significant change in our thinking.

If there was one word that described my childhood, it was confusion. How much dust was kicked up in the gravel driveway and the speed of the car would give us kids a clue if he had a good day. I was a little girl gripped by fear. I did everything I could do to protect my younger brothers. We could never figure out what would set him off. Dad was angry and physically violent. I remembered gathering my little brothers like a mother hen gathered her chicks and we would try to find a closet to huddle in until it was safe.

In reality, nowhere was safe. Childhood equaled fear.

Mom was mentally ill and always at odds with somebody in the family. Her type of mental illness destroyed relationships. I learned to cook early to feed my brothers. I did my best to clean the house, but there were always piles of unfolded laundry. One of the weird things about Mom was that she would compete with me. An uncle gave me a compliment about my appearance when I was a teenager. She didn't speak to me for a month. Mom didn't want me to tell anyone how old I was because just maybe they could figure out how old she was. I would miss four to six weeks of high school staying home to care for mom every year. Dad told me that if I didn't, he wouldn't be able to work. She was a master at pushing his buttons. He never lifted a finger against her. Us kids suffered instead. I made up stories about the bruises he inflicted. I remember when my father put his fist through the wall. He put a chair's legs through the ceiling. It was so strange to see it just hanging in thin air. I remember hiding beneath the piano hoping that he would calm down enough so I wouldn't get another beating.

I've struggled with fear for too much of my life.

Childhood was surreal. I was never good enough. I was sure everything was my fault. I was certain that I was responsible for the chaos. I wanted to be invisible. No one knew what was happening. There were no words to describe the turmoil I felt. My grandfather told me I wasn't good enough for college. There was never enough money. I cried myself to sleep and learned to pray.

It took decades to unravel and understand the abuse and its effects on me as well as my siblings. My brother closest in age was murdered just before his 21st birthday. He was trafficking drugs and had been dishonorably discharged from the Navy. My next younger drug addict brother spent most of his life homeless or in jail. He followed in my father's footsteps abusing his lovely wife and tormenting his children. Emotional scars never seem to heal.

Miraculously, my youngest brother became a talented neurosurgeon. His genius has blessed many patients in the operating room. I was trained to be a successful planner.

I understand why some people use drugs and alcohol to deal with the pain and suffering of an abusive childhood. I believe that abuse create holes in our psyche which we feel compelled to fill. This is where addictions start. There is no end to the types of addictions we use to fill these cavities.

I discovered God when I was in kindergarten. A friend invited me to a Good News Club. That's where I heard the Gospel for the first time. On a simple flannel graph board that told the story of how God sent his only son Jesus to Earth. If I trusted and believed in Him, then when I died that I could go to heaven. At five years old I knew that I wasn't always a good little girl. I understood that Jesus could forgive me. I am convinced that my relationship with God saved me.

It was the most important decision of my young life and has continued to be a central focus as an adult.

I was excited to be leaving for the weekend. I had signed up for a spiritual conference called Healing is a Choice. Three days without a husband or kids. This was a rare event indeed. The night before I left, after the kids were in bed, my husband and I had a conversation. He was concerned about my behavior and thought it was too controlling with our kids. I usually listened to Brad out of respect. He has tremendous discernment and insight. But this wasn't one of those times. I was excited and wasn't interested in his observations. I was getting away!

It was a great time Friday evening and all day on Saturday. A seminar workshop and learning atmosphere busy with large and small group sessions. Saturday evening the organizer led us in a time of praise and worship. He encouraged us to spend time in prayer or meditation. I had experienced a great time of renewal and encouragement. I was in a happy and relaxed state of mind. It felt as if the entire world was at peace until suddenly a thought entered my consciousness. Instant Divine clarity. As a Christian, I believe that it was God speaking to me. For others it's the universe or a higher power. But whatever, I was definitely not the origin of this realization. Without any warning I understood that I had unhealthy controlling behavior directed at the kids because of my murdered brother. I perceived this behavior was connected to a subconscious fear that I could lose one of my children.

Instantly, I could visualize how this fear was driving my behaviors. I was grateful for the prolonged silence that allowed me to process this rational reasoning. I finally understood this thought process had to change for my mental health as well as my relationship with our children who were precious to me. I will never forget this moment or the impact it has had upon the rest of my life. I immediately understood that there was almost nothing I could control and worrying and trying to exercise my willpower over any situation was futile and useless. At this moment the world was hushed and breathlessly still, allowing me to take pause. I made an important decision that night to create a habit of praying and intentionally letting go of my worries and fears that were hurting me and most likely driving my kids crazy.

It's normal to want to feel that we are in control; however, this need for control is fueled by fear. In life there are so many things that can go wrong. As mothers, we have a lot of anxiety when we are raising our children. We want them to eat right, to have a good education, to be healthy, to be happy, well-adjusted children experiencing normal relationships. When we are kids, we don't have control over our lives and can try to overcompensate by controlling our behaviors. But when we grow up in a dysfunctional family where things are quite unpredictable there can be an additional dimension. Exercising control gives us a false illusion of security and safety which can make us believe that by our sheer willpower, we can impact the circumstances with which we are coping. This kind of thinking is a lie.

That night I made an important decision to create an awareness of the things that were of a concern in my life: all my worries and anxieties. First to identify them and second to pray and release them. This was not an easy task. I apologized to Brad. He was right. I apologized to the kids and promised to make changes in my behavior.

Day after day, I would pray. After I prayed, I would see an image in my mind that I was physically putting these worries on an altar. But as I walked away, I saw myself dragging these cares back with me. It was ever so clear that I was not releasing the very things in my life that were influencing my behavior. I was grateful for this visualization and recognition that I wasn't dismissing these anxieties and fears. I never stopped praying and I was determined not to give up. I kept doing my best to create this new habit. Many months later the altar image disappeared. I felt at peace as I became aware that this change was finally happening. I was beginning to release the things that were plaguing me. Not that it's easy and not that there haven't been times in my life when I back slide into worry and fear. But this new awareness and habit stayed with me year after year.

I was experiencing freedom and it was grounding me. I was consciously releasing my fears and anxieties. I needed to slow down enough to create the awareness and then intentionally pray to release them. Since then, I've learned the importance of daily meditation. It's natural to try and control people and our environment, but exercising control gives us a false sense of security and safety, because feeling we are in control is a false reality. The reality is that it's impossible to control the majority of things that occur in life. And it's definitely impossible to control other people. Exercising control does not make our lives better. Becoming controlling creates a multitude of problems, adds stress to our lives and makes our relationships more difficult to manage and enjoy.

Everything became bright and clear once I understood that I couldn't control events or outcomes. The only thing I can control is my response to them, and that's what I keep working on. This was the habit I needed. Giving up control has been a fascinating journey and has allowed me to have much more freedom. I don't have worries weighing down my mind. I have more clarity and I am able to process life so much better. I have accepted the truth that there is almost nothing I can control. This discovery has been one of the biggest influences of my life.

The only constant in the universe is change.

Life will present challenges, and the unexpected will happen. Giving up control and learning to let go has been the most freeing of anything I've ever done. I'm so much happier and am experiencing much more joy and peace. My relationships are deeper and more meaningful. I can handle stress better. I'm more relaxed and at ease. I have become vulnerable and transparent. I am more compassionate with others because the focus isn't on me. I'm practicing releasing my burdens and living in gratitude every day. I am very aware that living this way is allowing me to be more present with my family and others. This realization has changed the way I live. It has changed the way I think. It has changed my behavior.

This transformation is allowing me to experience a much richer and deeper life. The best part is that I no longer have these worries, fears and anxieties taking up space in my brain. As a result, I have the freedom to be more creative. I am watching my goals gracefully unfold and becoming a reality.

I'm choosing to live my life with forgiveness, grace, hope and mercy with more love. I've learned to let go. Life can be a blessing and full of joy. ✿

Notes

Robin Eldridge Hain

Robin's successful thirty-year career with Colgate-Palmolive developed her practical skills that provide solutions to social challenges.

Robin has studied current practices in the field of addiction through the American Society of Addictive Medicine. Robin completed Family based Family facilitator training through Nami and SOS Recovery Community. Robin's mission is to end stigma and advocate for policy changes that support long-term recovery systems of care. RecoveryStrongCommunity.org platform is under development to meet this mission. Five-year board service: www.MWVsupportsrecovery.org and www.sicd-fl.org.

Robin is one of the 30 women authors in Jan Fraser's Inspired Life Series *The Book on Joy*. Her chapter "Fearlessly Choosing Joy" brings hope in the most challenging of times. She and her husband, Scott, reside in Sarasota, Florida and Silver Lake, New Hampshire. They enjoy traveling the world and cherish time spent with family and friends.

Contact
Website: www.robineldridgehain.com

Advocating for Change

By Robin Eldridge Hain

*"The power of transformation takes away
the old and gives the new."*

— Angel Card

Mental illness and the disease of addiction fluttered in and out of my life. This story is about the journey of transformation that occurred from my childhood experiences, through college and as I became a mother. These challenges on my journey transformed me from a witness to an advocate.

Our children are watching how we cope with day-to-day life.

I grew up in a close loving family that gathered together at least once a week to share Sunday dinner around the dining room table. My grandparents were the glue that kept this tradition alive. The aroma of pot roast, cheap wine, and Budweiser filled the air. My grandfather was in his early forties when his job brought on anxiety and depression. Electric shock therapy reduced his symptoms. Later in life he found a shot or two of vodka had the same effect at calming his nerves.

My mother and her friends would talk about the wonders of valium to get a good night sleep. Scotch or wine accompanied many of her evening meals. Her two brothers also found comfort from the liquor store. In fact, all of her siblings had bouts of depression and died early from various cancers.

My psychology major was the beginning of my search for healthier solutions to life's challenges. Procrastination increased my anxiety, yet it seemed that my productivity was at peak performance when I was pulling all-nighters to prep for exams and finish papers. Then I'd crash. Then I'd party. I always felt like I had more fun and danced better after of few glasses of wine, but depression would inevitably set in, and the cycle would repeat throughout my four years of college.

Throughout my adult life I sought individual therapy for anxiety and depression. I discovered the benefits of meditation and yoga as healthy alternatives to medication. A glass or two of wine was a nightly relaxation ritual. In my marriage, drinking was what we did to relax and to celebrate. Drinking in the evenings was our normal. At the time it seemed a harmless habit.

At this point in my life, there was only one relationship missing. I always wanted children, but I could never imagine the intense emotion of becoming a parent until it became a reality. I was filled with overwhelming joy when my wish was fulfilled and we welcomed our son, Nevin, into our family. I felt the weight of the responsibility of caring for this little soul. I thought I could protect him. I vowed I would never let anything happen to him.

Transformation through Education

Looking back, I learned at an early age that I could overcome. In sixth grade, I struggled with anxiety. My poor academic performance led to a reading evaluation. I was asked to read all the words on the page into a microphone and it would type out each word that I read: "the, they, ran, in and so on." This is when it was discovered that I had not learned to read. I met twice a week in a tiny room with the reading specialist and the reading machine. By the end of sixth grade, my comprehension was at grade level. Confidence replaced my anxiety, and recreational reading became a new hobby. The turn of each page expanded my world and just like that – my school life was transformed by that intervention.

Sixth grade was also a transformational time for my son. Before this time, our family life revolved around school, sports and time with family and friends. Strangely, his school performance began declining, and school personnel described him as being more present in the hallways than most of the other students. Professional evaluations resulted in a diagnosis of ADHD, anxiety, and depression. I did not see the characteristics of these labels, but I trusted the professionals and agreed to administer medications. The medications made it harder for him to wake up in the morning and to stay awake during the school day. He started to change. My biggest fear was that these medications would only teach him to seek out recreational substances to help him feel better. The reality was he started his own experiments on ways to feel better. His interest in playing sports began to diminish. Monthly medication monitoring led to more medications and so began the downward spiral of Substance Use Disorder or SUD.

Little did I know how much I would learn about this condition, its causes, symptoms and remedies in the future.

Nevin continued to struggle. He was in high school when the disease of addiction hijacked his brain. You may have heard that addiction is a family disease. It has a way of challenging even the strongest of families, and it was no different for us.

Thankfully, the online education process allowed my son to graduate from high school. It was much more productive than the alternatives. During this ten-year journey, our family has cycled through remission, recovery and relapse. We went through days and nights when we didn't know if our son was alive or dead – that is one of the toughest experiences a parent can face.

As any mother of a child who suffers from addiction knows, it is too easy to blame yourself. I've often thought that if I had a do-over, I would not have taken the medication route with him. I do believe that medication has a place when someone is climbing out of their skin, delusional, or just can't shake that dark cloud. But for Nevin in the sixth grade, I realize I was too quick to trust the 'professionals' instead of standing up for the son I knew and looking for alternatives. I also would have encouraged him to stay in sports. Too often I hear people in recovery remark that leaving extracurricular sports is their biggest regret.

When it came to drinking alcohol, I realized that he had witnessed my nightly glasses of wine at dinner with or without company. He had attended those family gatherings where drinking was the standard activity. In fact, in early recovery, celebrating his Anniversary, my son had a beer. He said he wanted to be like everyone else and have a beer to celebrate. He just wanted to be normal. That was the beginning of his relapse.

I have participated in family support groups over the last 10 years. This community of families experiencing the trauma of a loved one in active addiction has helped me regain my sanity, set boundaries and build tools for self-care. I learned that unconditional love is a key component to recovery.

In the last decade I have studied many pathways to recovery. I have consulted with multiple educational and behavior health professionals. My library continues to grow. I follow leading organizations in the field of mental health, substance use disorder, and alcoholism. I watch webinars and online programs on the latest treatments.

I advocate for policy changes that can end the stigma and promote oversight of licensed treatment providers. I advocate for change and transformation for our youth, young adults and anyone afflicted with this disease.

My view of the world has been transformed by what I witnessed, what I did, and what I did not do. If you are in this, or a similar situation, take heart. The key is to never give up hope. Today, he is a contributing member of society. I am grateful for his arrival here. The power of unconditional love and fellowship organizations offer aid along the many pathways to recovery.

Today, when I see a baseball player, I see my son. When I see a homeless person, I see my son. When I see a person in recovery, I see my son.

Self and Community Transformation Advocacy

I believe each of us has the power to grow and change. Advocacy for change starts with all individuals, families and community members that have been impacted by the disease of addiction. Walking through the valley of addiction as a witness or victim empowers us with the strength to pave unplanned pathways.

I believe connecting detox and treatment centers to medical facilities reduces stigma and achieves parity care to medical health by treating the whole person. Sober living housing within the community promotes family education and engagement. Drug labeling and addiction education for all prescribing professionals will reduce medical related gateways to addictive medications.

I believe K-12 school systems that utilize resource officers and mental health professionals build healthy relationships with the student population and provide key coping skills and trauma intervention. Addiction curriculum integrated with health, fitness and science classes offers cohesive messaging for prevention. Everyone wins with a Recovery Strong Community.

Ilka V. Chavez

Ilka is a #1 international best-selling author of several books and a fervent leader with an extensive track record for helping individuals, communities and organizations transform and reach their highest potential. She is a lover of people and life and is dedicated to mentoring and guiding people and organizations to identify and activate the leader within. She is a strong believer that following God's design is the perfect blueprint for authentic leadership. Her goal is to awaken the masses and help them create and lead a life they love living every day.

She is the President of Corporate GOLD LLC, a leadership consulting, training and coaching company. She is a certified emotional mastery, life mastery, and transformational executive coach, and an international inspirational speaker. She is passionate about leadership, transformation through trusting the process and leading in excellence. Her slogan is "Learn It, Live It, Lead it!"

Contact
Websites: www.ilkavchavez.com and www.corporate-gold.com
Email: ilka@corporate-gold.com

Transformation – The Fiery Trials of Becoming

By Ilka V. Chavez

"We must endure the fiery trials of transformation to become our best selves and to ignite transformation in others."

— Ilka V. Chavez

Before you arrive at a destination you may journey through some trail, driveway, footpath, walkway, path, passage, an avenue or even a fiery trial or two. You don't awaken instantly and smoothly arrive to an envisioned location. One doesn't attain transformation all of a sudden. Transformation isn't magical; it doesn't happen by chance. It requires intentional and conscious action to become the best version of yourself, so you can say, "I know who I am, I know where I am, I know why I am here, and I love the life I am living."

"A transformation occurs when we go beyond the bounds of our current understanding and awareness. We cannot think our way through this change; we have to experience our way into it."
—Jim Marsden

Every human has the ability to transform. The process of transforming brings out fear, anxiety, confusion, disorientation, and may even feel like an out-of-body experience. This is the first sign that a storm may be ahead. During my triple storm of 2016 (cancer, marriage dissolution, and confusion about a twenty plus year career at the time), I held my first conference entitled, *"What Leaders Say and Do: How to Inspire your Tribe."* I created a presentation entitled *"Taking off the Old and Putting on the New."*

The last slide of my presentation was a picture of me and my family riding the rollercoaster at Universal Studios. In the first photo we were all scared and covered our eyes. The second photo, a year later, showed our hands in the air, buckled-in and smiling. I made the analogy that this is like life. I said, "Sometimes, we must simply buckle up, throw our hands in the air, smile and say Wheee." I think this was my soul preparing me for what was to come.

Unbeknownst to me, I was about to embark on this very process of transformation, abandoning the old me and allowing the molding and forming of the new me. One of rebirth and journey to my true identity.

My triple storm of 2016 felt like a whirlpool – a tornado in the middle of my life. It shook me to the very core. I was in the midst of what had become a toxic marriage that was killing my mental health and self-esteem, not to mention damaging my amazing children. Subconsciously, rejection and Imposter Syndrome were plaguing my identity. At the same time, I was diagnosed with cancer while leading a demanding high-level team as the Chief of Operations of the National Vaccine Program Office in Washington D. C. I had also recently been elected to a local school board position.

Every new life event triggers a form of transformation. It is up to each individual to drum up the courage to step into the fiery trial to transform over and over again. This ability makes it possible for a weak person to become strong; a fearful person to become courageous, and an immature person to mature. The ultimate reward of enduring this fiery trial is peace, one that surpasses all understanding. If only I knew this at the start of the trial . . . that, like the caterpillar, what I thought was the end, was actually the beginning of stepping into a greater, better version of myself.

I was able to find peace through my transformation. In the process of my marriage ending, I beat cancer, stepped down from the school board and reduced my hours at my job. I survived and was able to move forward as a stronger person. And I believe you can as well.

I now recognize when these transformations are forthcoming, we simply need to 'Buckle Up'. You arrive at one form of transformation and then there is another and another. The evolution never ends. For me, it means another turn or deep drop in my evolution, my journey of transformation, my journey of becoming.

Transformation is simply the act of becoming better or as I like to refer it as 'living in excellence.' Be better today than you were yesterday; be better tomorrow than you were today. It is the modification of an individual's personality by the incorporation of certain qualities, attitudes and habits that results in a change in a person's life and potentials.

Transformation usually starts internally. Consider your own personal transformation(s). Most likely, the process started from inside you and the effects flowed out to everything you were, did, and said. Your life changes as you change, only if you allow the process to flow. The things around you move in agreement to the way you think of them. It is about progressive alignment with your highest potential.

Vision and Transformation

The ability to envision transformation in one's heart is the beginning of being transformed. The presence of vision in the process provides strength, encouragement, and calm even in the midst of the storm.

I recall that what kept me pressing through my fiery trials of transformation was the vision and desire that my children learn from the experience. Thankfully, their faith is intact and their scars are minimal. This vision and longing gave me the strength to speak about my journey of transformation and write in books about this very painful process as I was vividly experiencing it. It was a true gift to journal in what I call 'En Vivo' aka 'Live.'

Leading Others through Transformation

Trials and tribulations are part of life and are unpredictable and inevitable. The word trial means an opportunity to test something.

Tribulation on the other hand means adversity, a trying period or event. Some trials and tribulations may last only for a season or others may not. Therefore, we shouldn't be discouraged when faced with challenges. Instead, as leaders, we need to be able to overcome these difficulties, persevere, and become better. These events are essential for our growth and are meant to push us into greatness despite the discomfort.

Truthfully, transformation doesn't only apply to self. It is not a process to be experienced alone. Instead, as you tread the path, you can transform others as well. In many ways, it is not wholly about you . . . it is also about those that surround you, those in your tribe and those that are coming behind you.

When gold is purified, it is usually put in a blast furnace that can produce a very high temperature. The blast furnace can be likened to trials and tribulations. But notice that when the gold comes out of the blast furnace, it glistens, and everyone wants to have it. In the same way, trials and tribulations can bring out the best in us. My fiery trials allowed me to better lead myself and my tribe.

"If you want to awaken all humanity, then awaken all of yourself, if you want to eliminate the suffering in the world, then eliminate all that is negative in yourself. Truly the greatest gift you have to give is that of your own self-transformation." — Lao Tzu

Change and transformation are an ongoing part of life. For some it is subtle for others it is dramatic. Transformation usually involves some discomfort and may involve pain. Remember that transforming and change is a process and not a destination, some parts of the process are easy and some not so easy. Embrace the process.

Becoming the best version of yourself may be triggered by a major life event, an awareness that you desire more, a longing or a discontent, or a loss of something or someone. The simple act of sharing genuine love and concern for others can also be transformational. I believe that God gave me a spirit not of fear but power and love and self-control. No matter what situation we face, we can be confident that God is with us, there is no need to fear.

Keep your destination in focus while you enjoy life's journey.

"A woman is the full circle. Within her is the power to create, nurture and transform." — Diane Mariechild

LouAnne Hunt

L ouAnne is a Canadian Keynote Speaker whose down-to-earth humour compels audiences to laugh while they learn. After thirty-six years, she retired from her government job. A second career in teaching the fundamentals of Business to thousands of adult students as a College Professor allowed her to polish her presentation skills. She has made a name for herself as a sought-after speaker, teacher, and Personal Development Coach.

Additionally, LouAnne is an award-winning entrepreneur, putting into practice what she teaches every day. She is a Certified Canfield trainer in The Success Principles™ and a Diabetes Prevention Program Lifestyle Coach.

LouAnne is using this opportunity to enhance her passion to work with pre-diabetes and Type 1 diabetics live a healthier lifestyle connecting their body, mind and spirit through guided meditation and wellness coaching.

If you are interested in having LouAnne work with you, in a group or as a motivational speaker, connect with her through her website.

Contact

Website: www.louannehunt.ca

Releasing the Weight

By LouAnne Hunt

"To transform yourself, you don't need to do big things. Just do small things in a big way. Transformation will follow you!"

— Rahul Sinha

You should have been there to see the look and disbelief on my face as I listened to the doctor tell me over the phone that I officially had type 2 diabetes in September 2020! My A1C was 7.9 (over 126 in the USA). A1C is a glycated hemoglobin or blood test that measures blood sugar levels over a 3-month period and is used to monitor and diagnose prediabetes and diabetes. A normal reading is anything below 5.5 in Canada and 85-99 in USA.

The doctor immediately prescribed a medication that I was to start right away. I asked her if I would have to take this prescription for the rest of my life. Her reply was "Yes!" She went on to explain, "Your mother was a diabetic, your sister is a diabetic, and you are diabetic too."

I was so disappointed in myself.

I started the medication right away because it was what the doctor ordered for me. Not doing well on that medication is an understatement. I was experiencing every side effect listed on the medication's pamphlet. After explaining to the doctor how I was feeling during a follow-up visit, she prescribed a different medication. Things didn't change for me, and I had to start taking 100% responsibility for myself and my attitude towards becoming healthy. It wasn't easy for me, and I knew the road to transformation was going to have a few bumps along the way.

Growing up, I was always the fat girl in school. I remember finding a baby picture and I was even fat in that picture. When I asked my mother about it, she said, "Oh yes, the doctor used to ask me what I was feeding you because you were so chubby." But it seemed to be okay with my mother because it was described as baby fat.

The unbelievable pressure to exercise more and eat less to lose weight came from my doctor, my family, my friends and even from my teachers. I thought they wanted me to lose weight so that I would be more lovable and acceptable.

When I was 16, I thought I was in love with an 18-year-old boy. We got engaged so that we could get married right after I was finished high school. Looking back, I can see how foolish I was to believe that this was the man of my dreams.

One day, we went to an amusement park in Sandusky, Ohio, called Cedar Point. While we were walking around, we decided to stop at a booth where a person was guessing participants' weight. I begged Mr. Weight Guesser to make sure that my fiancé didn't see the result on the scale. To win the tiny stuffed animal, I had to prove this guy was wrong in his guess. He was very kind and said a low number "125 pounds" out loud which is more in line with my 5'4" frame. Shaking as I stepped on the scale trusting that he would somehow camouflage my real weight, the needle quickly spun around to 160 pounds. Everyone who was standing in line behind me including the love of my life saw where the needle landed. Yes, I won the small stuffed animal, but I was horrified that everyone had seen those numbers on the scale. That is what started my unhealthy weight-loss and gain journey.

The relationship with my fiancé came to an end after graduating from high school and I began working three different shifts as a 9-1-1 dispatcher. Working in that job taught me a valuable lesson about Post Traumatic Stress Disorder (PTSD) and depression. On my

25th birthday, I was in my apartment watching television when a huge wave of sadness and loneliness came over me. I remember seeing only darkness. It felt like I was spinning and falling into a dark hole. It was the scariest moment of my life. I finally came out of that space and had no idea what had happened. I couldn't remember anything, but it was like a switch had been turned on inside of me ... a switch to eat. That is exactly what I did. I ate to fill that dark hole, trying to fill the feeling of loneliness, junk food became my friend. Seemingly out of nowhere, I quickly added 40 new pounds to my body.

My life became a constant adventure searching out the latest diet promising me to lose the unwanted pounds. You name it, I tried the new, old and the greatest. The grapefruit diet, the Scarsdale Diet, the Revolving diet, Calorie Counters, Weight Watchers, TOPS (Take off Pounds Sensibly), one meal per day, no meals, Eat for Life, Eat for your blood type, and so many other programs. If I read about it in a tabloid or magazine, I tried it. Sometimes I would have success but most of the time it was short-lived. I lost 10, 20, and 30 pounds only to gain the weight back plus more. I was always on a diet, starting a new diet, or researching the next best weight loss program. This would continue well into my fifties.

When I retired in 2017, I became a part-time college professor. Teaching business courses and personal development became my passion. I learned so much about myself and the importance of goal setting, intentions and finding my life's purpose from the things in my life that brought me joy. What affected me most was learning the art of gratitude and putting myself first. If you want to learn about yourself, your thoughts, and beliefs, teach them to someone else. I finally realized what was missing in my weight loss game.

What made this journey different than all of those in the past? My focus was on a different place. Now it was about getting healthy and reversing the diagnosis of Type 2 Diabetes, not having to take medication, and feeling like a normal person again. I wanted to feel more alive, not so tired, and not in constant pain. This time was different, my attitude towards myself had transformed. I finally put myself first knowing that everything and everyone in my life would benefit from the changes. It was so freeing, and it gave me a purpose.

I immediately set up a new gratitude journal to record my journey with the rule that only positive entries could be made. Nothing negative about how I was feeling, which way the scale was heading, or any reasons the plan was not followed that day. At the bottom or top of each page is an inspirational quote written in red.

My journal entry dated September 11, 2020:

So today is the day that I will start my journey, my journey to transformation.

Next blood work appointment: December 11, Goal is to weigh less than today and lower A1C reading to less than 6.5.

Three months from now you will thank yourself!

I researched the internet and hired a certified health coach to help me understand how my body was about to transform. She helped me understand how food affects my daily glucose levels, we had weekly check-ins to answer any questions, and she was my accountability partner. I was so inspired by my health coach that I became a certified Health and Diabetes Prevention Program coach to help as many as I could with their back to health journey.

It was important to make a commitment to myself in writing with a date and signature. I created graphs and hung them on the back of my door in my office to record the changes in my weight and body mass index (BMI). I found a great resource program to help me understand the difference between diabetes type 1 and type 2. The program helped me to set up a diabetes reversal plan that included a food and meal plan that worked best for me.

Find a food plan that works best for you. A food plan that is going to be pleasing to your palette but one that is sustainable for the long haul. For more information about health coaching, and the food plan please reach out to me.

My health coach introduced me to the concepts of intermittent fasting. She explained that if I could stick to a schedule of eating between 10:00 am and 6:00 pm I would be able to control my blood glucose levels throughout the day. When I first started this new way of eating, 25 grams of sugar, limiting my carbohydrate intake to 40 grams per day, and eating between 10:00 am and 6:00 pm I thought it wouldn't be possible, but it became my new way of life!

Short walks are an important part of becoming mobile again. I enjoy a leisurely walk outside for twenty minutes but when the weather is inclement, I use my treadmill and my stationary bike weekly to keep my body moving. Having a fitness tracker helped me keep track of everything including food, steps, and workouts. Find what works for you. I play walking and running videos that I find on YouTube during my walks or bike rides that make my workouts fun and interactive. These are great mind-hacks as I call them. I walk along the ocean in Florida or take a bike ride up the side of a mountain in Spain from my living room!

Adding daily meditation to my fitness routine has proved to be invaluable. Every morning when I first wake up or while I'm falling asleep at night, I play relaxing guided meditation recordings. It is proven how regular meditation lowers our resting heartrate, lowers the body's main stress hormone known as cortisol, helps curb cravings and hunger pangs. Meditation is just as important as exercising. Think of it as fitness for your brain.

It was time to create my intentions, so I created a vision board featuring pictures of a scale reversing diabetes, added an arrow pointing downward, and a picture of a blood drop with the words "Beat Type 2" printed across it. Inside the blood drop picture, I added the words "Below 6.5 Before Dec 11". This board hangs above my desk in my office so that I can read it every day and visualize myself being healthier and happier. When I attended the clinic to have my blood tested on December 11, I told the nurse about my goals and my vision board. She laughed and suggested not to get my hopes too high. When my results came back, my A1C was 6.0, dropping 1.9 points from 7.9 just 3 months prior.

One year later, on September 27, 2021, I reflected on my journey so far and celebrated the transformation I was making in my life. My journal entry reads:

Certified Jack Canfield Trainer, Certified Diabetes Prevention Program Coach, successfully following intermittent fasting eating between 10 am and 6 pm, walking daily with counts between 3000 steps and 5000 steps, A1C reading is currently 6.0 and I've released 50 pounds from my body.

As I write this, there are days when I am not 100% on the program and I try not to focus on the scale too much. When I need to transition back to taking control, I go back to researching the programs that I started on September 11, 2020. I would like to release more weight and I'm working towards that by setting new goals and believing in myself.

Your past is not who you are, your present is what you believe it is now. As George Eliot said, "It's never too late to be what you might have been."

Believing that making a transformation to a healthier me is possible, and I've proved that it's doable! ✺

Notes

JAN FRASER INSPIRED LIFE SERIES

Timely
TRANSFORMATIONS

Marjorie Lombard

Marjorie Lombard spent 60 years in the field of education, preschool through high school, recruited out of a college classroom to help meet the overflowing post-war school population in the mid 1950's. That meant greeting 50 fifth graders each morning during her first year of teaching. She has worked with students as a teacher and school administrator, in regular and special ed settings.

Currently she works as a volunteer with a small, independent school engaged in supporting homeschooling families and preparing to launch a membership website for parents and teachers, exploring new approaches in education. She is a writer and speaker on educational topics.

Contact
Email: lmedia518@gmail.com

Life Does Have Magical Moments

By Marjorie Lombard

"One moment can influence a lifetime."

– Marjorie Lombard

Have you ever had an experience, painful or awesome, which stunned you with a totally new understanding, altering forever your way of seeing your life, your possibilities, or even your way of viewing the lives and actions of others?

From one moment to the next, you were different and armed with a truth which would carry you through life's many painful or confusing moments with an ability to see the best in others, to hold out hope, and even to forgive.

One summer afternoon when I was ten, I went from pain to awe and to a totally new way of understanding what I experienced of the negative words and actions of others. My mother's simple response to my pain took me to a new level of consciousness and equipped me with an understanding and strength that would serve me well over seventy more years, and still does.

"Marjorie, would you take a quick walk to the store? I need a few more items for dinner."

"Sure, Mom. I'll take Tom and Colette with me."

For the moment I forgot what could happen when I took my six-year-old brother out for a walk. This was our first summer in the new neighborhood, but Tom had already experienced mocking and teasing. This wasn't the old neighborhood, where adults and kids just took Tommy for granted. They had seen his slow development, were used to his eager "conversation" with no words, since he could make sounds, but couldn't talk. The old neighbors had always been friendly and encouraging.

Tom was eager for the walk and Colette, a year younger, was happy to come with us. I took the shortcut to Beverly Glen Parkway, each of them by the hand, and we began the three-block stroll to the grocery store. The day was sunny and not too hot. I loved the color and fragrance of the flowers in our neighbors' yards.

Only too soon we heard shouts and mocking gibberish. Startled, we quickly looked back, just as two boys on bicycles spun by, swerving toward us as they passed, and laughing as we jumped back toward the picket fence. Tom began to cry, and Colette, frightened, clung to me. I pulled them both close, backs tight to the fence, as the boys, turning their bikes, careened directly toward us again, shouting and laughing, then swerving away and flying off with glee while continuing their mocking sounds.

Now both siblings were crying and I was pushing down fear and a sense of desperation. How to calm them? I hugged them both, tried to talk soothingly, then took their hands and continued, hurriedly now, walking to the store.

We took an alternate route home. By now Tom and Colette were seemingly calm. I settled them at their toys in the living room, took the grocery bag, and walked slowly toward the kitchen.

Mom was working at the sink, back turned. I silently placed the bag on the table and looked toward her, able now to let tears come to the surface. I couldn't speak. Mom stirred, looked back, then turned completely, potato and scrapper held at her sides.

"What – has happened . . .?"

I turned my head slightly from side to side, but still couldn't speak. Now the tears began to flow.

Mother took a step away from the sink. She looked searchingly at me. "Did those boys tease Tommy again?"

I nodded slightly, then I suddenly shouted, "Why! Why, Mom, do they do that?"

Mom lowered her arms, walked closer, set the potato and the scraper on the table. She looked at me for a moment longer and then said firmly but gently, "Marjorie, you have to understand something. We love Tom and we know that God has a purpose for Tommy's life. We will always love him and care for him.

"Those boys don't know any better. They don't understand. Their parents haven't taught them."

I felt suddenly calm as I took in her words, repeating in my mind . . . they don't know any better . . .

This was a revelation . . . they don't understand, they haven't been taught . . . I felt awe, as if those words were actually a truth I already carried somewhere inside. And Mom had given that truth words.

All the pain was gone. I was awestruck. There was a reason . . .

I didn't even go to my mother for a hug. I simply turned and walked off to be alone. The feeling of awe continued for some time. I had to ponder this idea, turn it around and around, make it part of my awareness, make it my own.

That truth has stayed with me for a lifetime. In later years I heard the same truth from another, expressed this way, "If men knew better, they would do better."

It has helped me to think the best of others even while knowing that their words and actions in a particular situation may be harmful or wrong. To see beyond the present when life seems too painful or confusing to endure. To restore a sense of hope if momentarily I lose faith in the future. Even to get through the pain of experiencing someone I love making a choice I don't want to believe he is capable of – on my part, getting through to acceptance – yes, this has indeed happened – getting through to peace and forgiveness.

It has taken me longer to apply this truth to myself, my own choices that I came to regret, my own words and actions I wish I could take back. Yet, to accept that we are still worthy of love and forgiveness, that in the moment we were choosing the best we could understand or the best we could muster under the circumstances – that is the real test of the truth, if she TRULY knew better, she would do better . . .

Transforming experiences take us to new levels of awareness and resilience. Sometimes the new awareness may be quite painful – accepting the reality of a situation in the present – that a relationship needs to be surrendered, that a love or acceptance we have yearned to have from a parent just isn't there, that an opportunity for achievement has escaped us. These moments can also be transforming as we accept, forgive, and move on, knowing that life still has hope and good things ahead.

When life hands us a magical moment, we can trust the truth of that moment and do our best to live it.

Notes

Myrto Mangrioti is a certified Canfield Trainer for the Success Principles & Methodology and a certified Deep Coach.

Music has a special place in Myrto's heart, which is why she worked as a Production Assistant, organising concerts all over the world for twenty years.

During her quest to find herself and the meaning of life, she dropped everything and founded Loving Living to pursue her passion for transforming the world, one person at a time.

Nature is her grounding place, and she feels energised by swimming all year round. One of her creative outlets is cooking, and she enjoys experimenting with new vegan recipes.

Myrto is the creator of the program "Playful Living Mastery". She believes life is a learning playground that shouldn't be taken too seriously. She loves helping people awaken to their true selves, enjoying their lives to the fullest by living in the present moment. She wants everyone to be the RockStar of their lives.

Contact

Websites: www.loving-living.com
www.deeptransformationalrockstar.com

A Good Girl's Quest for a Better World

By Myrto Mangrioti

"Your transformation enables transformation"

— Leon VanderPol

I always had a deep curiosity about life. I wanted to make sense of it. Why are we here? Where do we go? Where did we come from?

I remember being five years old, lying in bed and wondering about life. Having big dreams. I wanted to find the single cure to every disease. I wanted to find the secret to immortality. The secret to life. Usual five-year-old stuff! I remember having a great sense of purpose.

And then, real life happened. For one, my parents divorced. I could see how sad my mom was about the divorce, and it affected me deeply. Around the same time, I got bullied during my first year in Kindergarten.

I was plagued with questions: 'What did I do wrong?' 'Did I do something to deserve to be hit and teased by a boy at school?' 'Why did dad leave us?' 'Will something happen to mom too?' 'Are we gonna be all alone?' My mom and the school were very supportive, but I lost my sense of safety and stability.

I guess, there and then, I made the unconscious decision that what I wanted was to be a good girl. Not to cause any trouble or be in trouble. Be safe. I wanted to be loved and admired. I wanted to feel I was good enough. It became my mission. I got into automatic pilot, put up a brave face, always looking happy and positive. I did my best in every situation.

I was an A-student, the perfect daughter, President of my class, teacher's pet, and always helping classmates. I aced school. My mom was proud. She used to say, "I love going to school to see your teachers." They always ask me, "Why did you come? Myrto is doing great, and she's such a good kid." As for me . . . mission accomplished. My mom was happy!

As I grew up, I threw myself into different fields of learning and studying. A computer programmer, I could also talk astrology, do graphic design, teach things with ease, speed type, solve the Rubik cube. But I wasn't just into all the nerdy stuff. I could do sports too, like be a rally co-driver, ski, waterski, ice-skate, play tennis, scuba dive... and the list goes on. And boy, everyone loved my cooking (by the way, they still do)!

Anything that made me look good, I tried. And sometimes, it felt good too! But most of the time, it was exhausting.

My friends used to jokingly tell me: "You are a chameleon". And it was true! I could change who I was, depending on who I was with. At the time, I thought it was a compliment. It made me feel I was interesting to other people. But what a nightmare it actually was! Imagine, always having to play a role to get people to like you. I was constantly transforming but only on the outside.

It served my initial goal. To be a good girl and be liked.

As years went by, I changed different jobs, failed in relationships . . . and tried more and more to get a sense of satisfaction out of my life, but to no avail. I was feeling more and more lonely and less and less joyful. My self-esteem was going downhill.

At the age of 49, I hit rock bottom. My body started giving me signs I was not going in the right direction. I suffered from all kinds of skin diseases. I became overweight and depressed! My job only brought me stress, and nothing gave me satisfaction, except food, red wine and TV . . . or so I thought! I felt alone and disconnected from myself and everybody else.

That's when I had a panic attack. It was my wake-up call.

Newsflash: I had been unhappy for almost all my life. Always trapped by my "must do's" trying to be perfect and please everybody. For what? To feel liked and worthy. Well, it didn't work!!!

Being a good girl is no joyride. It sucks the life out of you!

I realised that even when I went out with friends or on vacation, I put so much pressure on myself to be who I thought everyone else wanted me to be. I could never relax and enjoy my free time! No wonder I always ended up needing time off, out of time off, to be by myself to recharge my batteries.

Somewhere along the way, I lost myself. I missed laughing. I craved to be carefree for once! I longed to fall asleep curled under the arms of a loving guy. I wanted a bank account that made me smile and not sweat with horror! I wanted to do something that gave meaning to my life. Something that I loved. And, I wanted to fit in my favourite jeans.

Everything screamed at me: Change!!

I took a leap of faith, and I did! It was not easy at the beginning. I had no idea what I wanted and liked when I was not trying to please someone else.

That's how lost I was. Then self-doubt came creeping in, 'What if they don't like me like that?' 'Am I good enough?' 'What if I fail?'

I searched deep inside myself to find my core values, my stability, my truth and this brought me peace. My word became authenticity, and my true transformation began. I started looking out for myself, taking care of MY wants and needs. If it did not feel authentic, I did not do it.

I stopped taking everything so seriously. I adopted a more creative and playful way of looking at things. I pushed myself to get out of my comfort zone. Tried out different approaches without scaring myself to death. I created new goals, taking one step at a time, always giving myself permission to pause, re-evaluate, even be lazy. And ask myself, 'Is this who I am, and is this what I want?'

And guess what I discovered?

I'm not meant to wait for "something" to be happy. The joy is in the ride. All I have to do is jump in wholeheartedly.

My ride has bumps along the way, but that's okay because nothing is a straight line. Everything is part of the game and the transformation, a learning curve. It's becoming more and more fun every day.

And guess what else I discovered?

As I am transforming, everyone around me has started transforming too.

First of all, their attitudes towards me. People I've known for years started treating me differently. People now get me and appreciate me, even when I'm not at my best, even when they don't agree with me. My relationships and connections are so much deeper and more fulfilling.

I can also see the shift in them. People close to me are getting things accomplished. I feel they are more present and aware. It's like the work I've been doing on myself is wearing off on them. And I'm thrilled. It was not my intention. My WHY was totally selfish. I wanted to be happy at last. Like the fairytale. But I guess this is one of the most beautiful and rewarding side effects of transformation! I just love it!

Now, I'm the Rockstar of my life. Front and centre, spreading love and joy around, curious and open in whatever comes next. Every day opens a new window to my transformation, be it tiny or a huge leap. Bring it on!

As I recall my childhood questions, I can now make sense of them. Maybe some don't even matter. It's all about the journey. It's about transformation and learning. It's about my life and the lives I touch along the way.

I have a purpose. I want to change the world. I don't want to see division, fear and hate. I long for peace, love, unity, creativity and joy. But, what I've realised is that true transformation comes from within.

My transformation began by finding silence, space and stillness within. Finding my inner-self, finding peace. Enjoying the small things in life.

Conversations over a glass of red wine or two, with good friends or a call with my mom. Having a hearty, loud laugh. Loving myself and my imperfections (not totally there yet!). Loving what is. Acceptance. Having an open mind and an open heart. Being present and aware. Listening. Giving my full attention to the NOW. Being in awe as I observe the ray of light shining through the leaves outside my window.

As I change, my vibration changes. My presence and all that I am move and resonate with my surroundings. I can sense it. Who isn't affected by everything and everyone they come in contact with?

Transformation is a work-in-progress. But it has a ripple effect starting from you and expanding to everyone around you. You can choose to be a positive or a negative influence. But consider this: Who doesn't want to be around some good vibes? Who doesn't feel better in the company of an open-minded, caring, positive being?

I invite you to join me in transformation, to make this world a better place. ✺

Lorraine Thomson

L orraine is an artist, teacher, trainer and seeker. After leaving a long career as a Nurse Practitioner, and completing an Honors Bachelor of Fine Arts, she is now following the path of her dreams as visual artist, and teacher of different creative processes and trainings. She is a life-long learner embracing new challenges and is a Certified Zentangle Teacher as well as Canfield Success Principles Trainer.

Whether Lorraine is working with intentional line and pattern drawing; using the non-dominant hand to write and paint; facilitating courses of *The Artist's Way*; or teaching the Success Principles, she uses her unique blend of various trainings in art, facilitation, creativity and health care to provide guidance, encouragement and skills to help people connect with their own creativity, and achieve more of what they really want in their lives.

Contact

Website: www.lorrainethomson.com
Email: lorraine@lorrainethomson.com

Your Head or Your Heart? What are You Listening To?

By Lorraine Thomson

"But all of the things we long for, are borne on the wings of change, and losses can lead us to blessings that we can't explain. Butterflies remind us, there's magic in every life, and we can become what we dream of, if fat furry worms can fly."

— from "Little Butterfly" song lyrics, Jana Stanfield

Maybe you can relate? In high school my highest grades and definitely, most favourite subject was art, though it was not thought by some to be a real career path. I was lucky to be in a big high school with a large variety of art classes with each focusing on a specific medium. I excelled in them and also in the sciences. My heart, and my passion however was art. I had been creative my whole life, always doing something – drawing, painting, coloring, illustrating stories, or making sculptural things.

I can clearly remember in Grade 13 when I had to make a head or heart decision about what I was going to be doing in post-secondary education. My parents made it quite clear that as their only child, I was going to University after graduation. My heart and love were dedicated to the arts. My art teachers were all questioning me as to why I wasn't applying to art schools whereas my science teachers, parents and guidance counsellors were saying the opposite, "Get a real job", "Art is only a hobby", "You'll be a starving artist", "Do something important", and "You can't make money as an artist!" Does this sound familiar if you were interested in the "Arts"?

When the time came, I made the decision to regretfully say 'No' to my heart and follow what my parents said. I was applauded for my decision. My heart and passion became like a sad, little mouse, dragging her heart, entering through a door, taking one last look, closing the door and locking it tight.

I left for Lakehead University in Thunder Bay to become a nurse. I had the sciences and math and did want to help people so that became my choice. While in University, there were art electives available, but I steered away from them because I knew if I got started, I would likely not want to stop. When you stifle something though, I believe it tends to squirt out in other ways. I learned to seriously knit during the University, not just scarves, actually full sweaters and cardigans with intricate patterns and cables! That was not enough to quell my inner art desires. I wasn't happy, dealing with depression in the third year of the four-year degree. In hindsight, I believe my body was trying to get my attention to have another look at the choices I had made, and maybe make different ones.

Unfortunately, I wasn't listening.

After 5 years I graduated with an Honors Bachelor of Science in Nursing. During my final year, I did a practicum in Northern Ontario, in fly-in Indigenous Communities working in a nursing stations. It was there I developed a taste for the expanded knowledge, duties and responsibilities of a Nurse Practitioner. I did further training and after working in the far north of Ontario for two years, I returned to Thunder Bay and worked as a Nurse Practitioner (NP) for eight years. By then there were life challenges, I was unhappy with a lagging interest in being an NP. I took a number of art courses over the years to try and appease that side of me but it wasn't enough. I always wanted more.

After moving to a smaller community in Southwestern Ontario, I kept finding myself drawn to nearby London, indeed, to take drawing classes through the local public art gallery. I continued the 45-minute driving commute for seven more years.

I wasn't particularly happy as something was always missing.

After reading books by Jack Canfield and doing personal growth work, I went to California in 2000 to do a week-long training with him to learn to teach his material. During the sessions, some emotional upsets were starting to percolate inside me. Doing a 5-minute speech about "Trusting Myself" loosened my emotions. Later that day, I met with assistant trainers and worked through my feelings and processes to clear them.

What came screaming out of me – I was an Artist! I needed to pursue this more. It was part of who I am, and I must do something with it.

When I got home, I felt a strong desire to go to the University and achieve the Fine Arts degree that I had always wanted to do. Many roadblocks were going through my head. 'Am I too old? Are my art skills too rusty? Can I do this? Does it cost too much? Will it take too much time? What was I thinking? Who are you to be doing this?' Those were all fears not truths. We need to feel the fear and do it anyway.

When you have a dream in your heart, I believe you need to follow it. It took a while but the idea wouldn't let go. I didn't want to go to my grave wondering if "I coulda, woulda, shoulda ?" At 37 years old, I started my adventure into the Fine Arts Program at Western University. Initially, I took one course at a time that would fit around my day job, loving every course and the chance to learn again in the University environment.

I was feeling stretched and unhappy so I tried changing locations again to a Health Centre in the city where I lived. I changed work days along with a life of twists and turns – marriage, moving homes, step-daughter living with us, helping both father and father-in-law with cancer treatments, an unexpected separation and divorce and life kept moving on. Seven years in, doing the courses and working almost fulltime, I was struggling again with burnout, depression, anxiety and now a new thing – panic attacks. On Sundays, the anxiety and unsettling feelings would start, sometimes it was the evening before or the Monday morning that a panic attack would happen as I prepared for work. Sometimes, it was a situation during the day like a disagreement among staff or an error in judgment. I questioned whether it would lead to burnout or do I make a change and make my heart sing? As I progressed, I realized more and more that I wanted a change. I had another big, head or heart decision to make. To complete the Fine Arts degree, I needed more extended studio time that wasn't possible with my current position. I had a stable, good paying career with great health benefits and prestige, AND I was miserable.

The populations I served over the years included teens, young women and children. One of the sad things I noticed was when I saw young people who had dreams that lit them up and excited them but important adults in their lives squashed their dreams and weren't supportive. I knew what that was like and how long or deeply it can affect someone.

In the end, I think we regret the things we didn't do rather than the ones where we went for it and may have not have fully succeeded. We still learned a lot along the way. I think our bodies give us signs – we often don't listen. If we are following someone else's path and not our own heart, we may find ourselves unhappy, unfulfilled or worse. I was following part of my dream working on the HBFA but still wanted more. Were there challenges and times I wanted to give up? Absolutely! I would then focus on why I wanted to do it, doing the spiritual work, journaling, and reminding myself of how I felt when I was creating. It's important to tell other trusted people about your dreams, enlisting help from your supporters when needed. I encourage you to follow your passion, put in the hard work and go for it.

At that time, I was reading a book* which suggested that when we needed guidance and answers about big questions, we could ask the Universe or God. It would be shown to us by receiving specific requested items in a time frame. I was losing sleep over the indecision – and making this request could change my whole life. I wrote in my journal and said out loud to the Universe my request, "If I am to quit being a Nurse Practitioner, show me a rose in 48 hours." I wrote it down but didn't tell anyone because the item has to come to you unbidden from the Universe.

---

*book "Sacred Signs: Hear, See & Believe Messages from the Universe" by Adrian Calabrese

Also, you don't specify how it will show up. If a family member gives you the thing because they know you want it, it isn't a sign from the Universe. Why a rose? I love roses, love drawing them and had recently done a very large pencil drawing for one of my university courses. I made my ask and I carried on as usual. I went to work the first day wondering how or if it would show up, and then forgot about it. As the day in the clinic got busy, no rose appeared that first day. The skepticism increased. I reasoned that I still had another day.

I went to work the next day as usual. The morning was steady and my first appointment after lunch was short and easy. The client who was a little late, came bustling in with a number of plastic bags from the dollar store, and we had our appointment. As she gathered her bags and headed out to the waiting room, I walked with her as I needed to get on with the next appointment. The client who was just about to leave, said quickly, "Oh wait, just a minute, I have something for you!" At this point I was anxious to get going with the next client, but waited as she rooted around in her bags, and pulled something out handing it to me. To my amazement, she pulled out a long-stemmed, yellow, artificial rose and gave it to me! I was stunned! I mumbled a thank you very much. "How kind of you," I said. I told the next client I needed a minute. I quickly walked down the hall into my office, shut the door and burst into tears.

My client had no idea what she had given me. I couldn't believe my eyes! Wow! I knew for certain then it was time to quit being a nurse practitioner. I somehow collected myself and finished working that afternoon. I knew it was imperative now – when you get a signal that clear, you must follow it. I was going to follow my heart this time! May the door be flung open to possibilities!

Through facing many fears and challenges along the way, staying true to myself and what I really wanted in the first place, I was able to complete and graduate at 46 years young with Honors, a Bachelor of Fine Arts Degree nine years after I started. Nine years! Although my father had passed 6 months before I graduated, my parents had come around and were again proud of me.

Looking back, I see that it took perseverance and guts to follow my heart. It was a bumpy road and was so worth it! I have no regrets!

After leaving the nursing profession, the panic attacks stopped. I was much happier and have loved creating art and helping other people find their creativity as well.

While I was working in my studio one afternoon where I teach and create, I was prepping for an upcoming workshop. As I played with some art supplies and looked around at my beloved space, I thought 'Wow! It's amazing that I get paid to do this! I love my job!' I had a huge smile on my face and as my sense of gratitude flowed, so did the tears.

What are you listening to? What dreams are being whispered from your heart? ✿

Notes

Barbara Blue

B arbara lives on The Wild Atlantic Way, in Connemara, Co Galway, Ireland. She lives with her daughter DeAnna. Both are native Gaelic speakers, something which is only still common in a few small pockets of Ireland called a 'Gaeltacht'.

Barbara has a BA Hons degree in English and Irish, from NUIG College, Ireland. After college she spent a few years in Milwaukee, US, and when she returned to Ireland she somehow found herself working in the world of accountancy and finance. She went on to do an online Diploma in Psychology and Counselling – probably to delve deeper into how she ended up working as an accountant! In order to remind herself of the 'inner author' she hoped was still lurking within, Barbara spent a few years writing scripts for a long-running Irish speaking (Gaelic) soap drama called Ros na Run, on top of her full-time finance job.

When Barbara is not avidly reading as many books as she can, she loves to cook, watch movies, and partake in just 'one or two' glasses of wine . . . since all bottles are made of glass after all . . .

Contact

Email: babsblue@gmail.com

Amazing Journey

By Barbara Blue

"Transformation is a journey without a final destination."
— Marilyn Ferguson

When I reflect on my life to date in relation to what I would consider my biggest transformative time to be, I believe the word 'Matrescence' sums it up. It's not a word I would have known at the time it began for me, but it means 'a woman's transition into motherhood'. For me, becoming a mother was definitely one of the biggest, and most rewarding transformations that I have gone through. I am still going through this today.

"Matrescence is not a biological event, it is a developmental process that takes time." — Nikki McCahon

Discovering I was pregnant did not happen at the most ideal time of my life. I was separated from my then husband, and had recently moved home to Ireland from the US. I was living with my parents while trying to get back on my feet and find a home of my own. It felt daunting and surreal and terrifying at times. I didn't realise that those feelings would continue into motherhood, long after the pregnancy and birth. However, it was also a time where a new love blossomed, a maternal love for the little being growing inside me. Suddenly I found my perspective on certain things and my sense of responsibility slowly transforming into something new. Something that would forevermore mean not just me and my life, but another person to always consider and factor into all of my thoughts, concerns and actions.

My ex-husband moved to Ireland for a time, and we tried to make things work because we had a baby to look after, but it didn't go the distance. So, the next part of my transformation journey went from motherhood, to single motherhood. It was now all me to be responsible for the raising of our gorgeous little daughter. A task that was such a rollercoaster of emotions including stress, anxiety, fear, loneliness and overwhelm. I was afraid I would never be enough, have enough, or give her enough. Surpassing those emotions were love, pride, joy and utter happiness at having such a wonderful little being to cherish and share my life.

Being a mother made me realise that I had no choice but to face my fears head-on. I no longer had an option to shy away from things that scared me, as I now had my daughter to consider in all things. I couldn't run away from being stressed about lack of finances or providing for her. I just had to find a way to make it happen! Being responsible for someone else's health and well-being is a huge commitment. The transformation in accepting the role of a parent and understanding the blessing it could be, was a life changer for me.

When my daughter, DeAnna, was still a baby, I would watch her with fascination at the fact that this amazing and beautiful being grew inside me. Granted, I suffered with sickness and heartburn throughout the pregnancy, and that wasn't much fun. Neither was the 33-hour labour, but her big brown eyes gazing into mine certainly made it all worthwhile! As she got a bit older, I marvelled at the things she would learn and do. Early on, she developed her own character and sense of humour. I had to adapt and transform along with her growth in order to facilitate the different steps and stages of her own life's journey.

"To describe my mother would be to write about a hurricane in its perfect power. Or the climbing, falling colors of a rainbow." — Maya Angelou

Another part of my own transformation into motherhood is the insight it now gave me into my own mother's thoughts and actions. Looking back on times where I had thought her harsh or critical as we were growing up, I could now see it as her being worried and concerned for us. Thinking back to how fastidious she always wanted our house to be, I could now see that it must have been so hard for her to keep on top of everything with all that she had to do.

My mother was a primary school teacher who taught over 40 children a day, and then came home to seven of her own. We were all within a ten-year age range from eldest to youngest. And yet, she found time to keep a very clean and tidy house, cook the most amazing dinners, bake wonderful cakes and pies, knit and sew clothes for all of us, and still have time to love my dad unconditionally. She raised us to live up to the best of our capabilities. Mom was a whirlwind of activity, able to multitask better than anyone I've ever known!

I was a challenging teenager, something I now regret as I realised I added to her stress and anxiety through my own teenage selfishness. I'm glad that my transformation into motherhood also brought a closeness between us that would never be shaken even after her death in 2011.

Janet Dickens wrote *"The wings of transformation are born of patience and struggle".* I can honestly say my mother bore those wings with an indomitable strength.

Watching DeAnna's own transformation, from baby to toddler, from toddler to child, from child to adolescent, and now to being an independent woman in her third year of college has been joyful. I've been blessed to be a huge part of her journey. There were ups and downs along the way, but thankfully the 'ups' were a lot more plentiful! We loved building a blanket fort and camping out in our sitting room when we couldn't afford to go anywhere. We had picnics on the lawn together and cosy movie nights snuggled up on the couch together, as we transformed into something a step further than just mother and daughter.

We developed a bond of friendship that is worth the absolute world to both of us.

I have learned throughout this transformation of motherhood you don't have to be a perfect mother to be a good mother, and you don't have to have a lot of financial wealth in order to gain a treasure of memories! I have also realised that the more you overcome various challenges in life, the more strength you develop to face future ones.

Recently, I learned that the collective noun for a group of mothers is a 'consternation.' That word taken on its own can convey fearfulness or dismay, and perhaps those are applicable to motherhood at times. I also read a quote that states 'being a mother is learning about strengths you didn't know you had, and dealing with fears you didn't know existed.'

I believe my transformation into motherhood gave me strength to face and overcome many fears, as well as show me total and utter love, fun, happiness, pride and joy that can come along with the amazing journey! ✿

Notes

Alynn Godfroy

A lynn Godfroy is a graduate of the University of Windsor and has an Honours Bachelor of Commerce degree.

She has been a Financial Advisor for almost 20 years and owns Godfroy Financial Management Ltd.

She is the author of "Why You Need a Financial Advisor" and has a 4-year old son, a husband and four stepchildren.

Alynn was a Rotarian for 11 years and served as the President of the Rotary Club of Belle River and is the Charter President of the area's newest club, the Rotary Club of Windsor-Walkerville. She has participated in volunteer missions to Venezuela where doctors and nurses performed cleft lip and cleft palate surgeries. Alynn has also been to Ghana three times helping to renovate two schools and a health clinic.

Alynn has served seven years as a board member of Community Living Windsor and is now on the board for ALSO (Assisted Living Southwestern Ontario).

Contact

Website: www.godfroyfinancialgroup.com

Careful Choices Create Future Freedom

By Alynn Godfroy

"A good financial plan is a roadmap that shows us exactly how the choices we make today will affect our future."

— Alexa von Tobel

In 2006 I had a life event that drastically changed my life. My partner at the time was working in a family business and the business was sold to another company. The new owners didn't want the family continuing to work for them so my partner was out of a job. In Canada when you lose a job you can normally qualify for unemployment and receive pay for up to a year however there are some restrictions and this includes when leaving a family business. We were suddenly down to one income and I went into full-on panic mode.

They say drastic times call for drastic measures and this was definitely one of those times in my life. In hindsight, I may have gone a little overboard, but I cut out absolutely everything that was not a necessity.

I stopped getting my nails done and did my own home manicures (saving $30 bi-weekly). I stopped going for my standing six-week hair appointment ($100 every 6 weeks). We cut out our Friday night pizza and wing nights ($40 weekly) and our Saturday night date night ($60 to $100 weekly).

Instead of going out for lunch with colleagues or clients 3 to 4 days per week I started bringing a lunch to my office ($60 per week). I had two gym memberships (one at a traditional gym and another at a kettle bell gym). I cancelled both of my memberships and started going for walks, bike rides, runs and did my own home workouts (saving $160 per month).

I used to stop for a coffee and bagel pretty much every morning before work. I started making coffee at home and making breakfast at home as well (saving $20 per week). We went to the most basic cell phone package ($30 monthly savings), the most basic Internet package ($20 monthly savings) and cut out our home phone ($53 monthly savings). Then we cancelled our cable TV ($80 per month).

Keep in mind this was before Netflix, Crave, Hulu, Disney+ etc. so it wasn't that hard to cut out these services. I think this would be a little harder to do today versus 17 years ago when I cancelled everything.

I used to go to Starbucks every couple of weeks and buy myself a fancy coffee and walk around the Chapters store that was attached to Starbucks. I am an absolutely voracious reader so I would spend anywhere between $50 and $80 each trip to buy books to read in the evenings and on weekends. I cut out that bi-weekly ritual and started walking three blocks down the street to the library (savings of $70 on average bi-weekly). Did you know that they have thousands and thousands of books there and you don't actually have to pay for them? I can't believe what that small change really did in terms of helping me to save money.

I was also in a women's bowling league and bowled every Wednesday night from September to May. I stopped bowling in the league and that saved me $15 per week plus I would usually have a drink or two and a burger or appetizer ($20 per week). This really helped me to cut down on spending.

In the summertime I played baseball and decided not to play the one summer and save myself the annual sign-up fee as well as the cost of drinks and snacks for my Tuesday and Thursday night game nights ($250 sign-up fee plus $40 per week on social outings from June to September).

If you're thinking wow that's a lot of money and trying to add it up, it was a savings of $19,986 and I was just getting started.

I was extremely fortunate during this time that my family was very supportive. I expressed that we were only down to one income, and I was concerned about my finances. Instead of going out for dinner for birthdays and occasions we took turns having dinner or BBQs at different family members' houses. We talked about money regularly in our household growing up, so I wasn't embarrassed to talk about my situation. Keeping an open dialogue about money has been one of my biggest successes with family and friends.

I was a Financial Advisor working in a big office where I paid $750 per month for rent. I decided to work from home to free up that cash. I saved $10,170 to be exact because there was GST on there that I was saving too. I already met with a lot of clients at their homes, so I didn't really need an office at the branch office. If I did need a meeting room, I just booked the board room. It also made it much easier to not spend money on lunches out with colleagues because we weren't all hanging around the office together then going for lunch.

I also increased my production levels because I was more effective working at home. I didn't have interruptions by having colleagues pop their heads into my office to say hello and the idle water cooler chit-chat was non-existent because I was working at home. I also had more time to do meal prep and make meals at home when I took breaks from working from home. I was not only working more methodically but this went hand in hand with being more efficient with my money.

Instead of going overboard on occasions like Christmas, birthdays, Mother's Day and Father's Day, I made gifts for my family or purchased low-cost gifts. Instead of taking my mom out for brunch for Mother's Day, I made her a nice breakfast which she appreciated much more. I made her a beautiful card with a picture collage and bought her lovely flowers at the grocery store and put them in a beautiful glass vase that I had found at a second-hand store.

This event in my life really shaped who I am today.

It may seem like I really restricted myself, but I didn't. I didn't go for my bi-weekly manicures at a salon but instead I put on music, poured myself a glass of wine and did my own nails at home.

I gave up a lot but this gal was not giving up her vino!

I cancelled my gym memberships and did a new workout routine in my basement. It saved me the driving time as one of the gyms was 15 minutes from my house. I took my dog on longer walks, rode my bike more and even attempted roller blading (well that was an epic fail as I am not that coordinated but I still tried it).

I found low-cost, amazing recipes online and really enjoyed cooking. We still did pizza night every week but instead we had home-made pizza. In place of date nights to the movies and going out for dinner, we had friends over and did game nights. I definitely learned to be more creative by inviting people over for meals and activities. We really did have more fun than we did by going out.

You may have heard the saying, "When you change the way you look at things, the things you look at change." Things changed and we had one less income coming into our household, but we still had a roof over our heads and we had transportation. We were grateful for our supportive family and our good health.

It didn't feel like it at the time, but we were really given a gift. In our society there are so many people merely collecting things. We became minimalists and we became more frugal out of necessity. One of my favorite quotes is from Dave Ramsey that says, "We buy things we don't need with money we don't have to impress people we don't like."

This is a gift and a mindset that I now share with friends, family and clients.

When I was in my early 20's, I was simply going through the motions and spending money. I was a Financial Advisor, starting to earn a good income. I really had to stop and look at how I was spending money on a day-to-day basis. I developed some habits, but I realized that I really didn't like the habits. Convenience had me buying a coffee and a bagel at a drive-thru on my way to the office. But, if I really thought about how much effort it took to go to the ATM, pull out cash to have for the week and then wait in line at the drive-thru, it was actually easier to buy bagels and coffee and prepare them at home. I not only saved money, I saved time. One might also argue that I wasn't running my car longer than necessary by sitting in a drive-thru. I gave up my office and worked from home so changing my morning routine was really easy.

I did a lot of 'self-reflection' to determine what was important to me. It was important to be active and healthy. I realized that I didn't need to spend $160 per month on two gym memberships to be healthy. I did groceries on Sunday mornings and cut up fruits and veggies, making healthy meals for the week and saving money in the process. I started riding my bike and taking my dog for longer walks. I found workout videos on You Tube that were free. My lifestyle didn't suffer because of this change. I actually gained 30 minutes every morning by not driving 15 minutes each way to the kettlebell gym. I utilized those 30 minutes to do journaling and planning out my day.

I found creative ideas online on low-cost gifts to make for friends and family for holidays and special occasions. I made picture collages accompanied by music one year for Christmas and I was overwhelmed by the tears of joy that my family shed when watching their person-alized videos. Keep in mind this was 2005/2006 so it was much more labour-intensive to put together a video than it is today. My family ap-preciated the thoughtfulness of the gift as well as the time and effort that I put into creating the gift. It was also something that they could keep and reflect back on in the future so it was really well received.

In my mid-twenties I was definitely handed some lemons but decided to make lemonade. I was determined to change the way I approached my routine every day and my relationship with money.

Fast forward 17 years later...I am now in my early 40s, remarried with a four-year-old son. We make 99 percent of our meals at home. I have scaled back the number of books I read in a month because I am busy building new creations out of Lego, doing puzzles and reading with my son. I still love reading and I continue to get books from the library. Now I also get them digitally so it is even easier than physically going to the library.

We still continue to make homemade gifts. It is more fun now that my son can help me do them. And the best website/app is Pinterest.

There are countless ideas on homemade gifts for Christmas, Mother's Day, Father's Day, etc.

I have been blessed with owning a business that I really love and enjoy. I talk about saving money and setting goals every day with my clients. When you get accustomed to living on one income and then you go back to having two incomes, it is easy to save a lot of money. I'm in the financial position now that I can retire by age 45. I definitely won't retire then, because I absolutely love what I do and it doesn't feel like work.

I'm sure you have heard the quote "If you love what you do, you'll never work a day in your life."

When I reflect on the journey I have taken over the past 17 years since this transformational event, I realize that I have refined one of my talents. The talent is my gift of being approachable and helping others get a handle on their finances and take back control.

My husband and I recently purchased our dream home out in the country where it is quiet and peaceful.

I am truly grateful for the lessons I have learned on this journey and the many teachers that have helped me achieve success. ❁

Notes

Janis Neary Miller

Janis Neary Miller lives a fulfilling life playing in the mountains of Utah, with her daughter, an aspiring "Doctor on the Moon;" her husband, an Army Medic; one very attentive Rottweiler and a flock of laying hens.

She has been everything from an IT geek to a 25+ year wellness coach and MLM entrepreneur. From an adaptive recreation manager to military support liaison, executive assistant, training manager, business strategist and beach bum, she's grateful for the winding path that led her back to her gift, passion and purpose that was always there – Intuitive Astrology.

Janis believes that astrology is a tool that can bring awareness to the energies that are divinely and uniquely you. Janis loves when clients connect to their own "inner G.U.R.U" – their Genuine Unique Real Unapologetic – Selves and purpose. Her readings and coaching help them to trust their inner wisdom, find healing through self-reclamation and to shine in their true purpose.

Contact
Website: www.guru-you.com

Turning Inward to Find My True Self

By Janis Neary Miller

"Only the truth of who you are, if realized, will set you free."

— Eckhart Tolle

I had spent countless hours and thousands of dollars to transform my traumatic and troubled childhood into a healthy and successful adulthood. From therapy to life coaches, and tons of personal development – I was intentional in creating a "normal" life. From an outside perspective, I had succeeded. I had an amazing husband and a vibrant, beautiful 4-year-old daughter. For example, last week's family pic on Facebook got over 180 likes. Most people guessed I was in my late 20's when I was over 40.

Even though I had given up the millionaire and the mansion in my last relationship, I was now building my own wealth in a beautiful mountain rural lifestyle . . . including an amazing cabin. My life still seemed influencer status worthy.

But it felt false. I was a fake. People didn't know. I was an imposter

I was determined to be different though. I had always worked on my mindset. Teachings from gurus and coaches' swirled in my head.

'Fake it until you make it. BE DO HAVE. Opportunities don't happen, you create them. Change your thoughts, change your life.' I did affirmations and went to countless personal development classes and read the books. I was a goal setter and a go-getter.

People were always saying, "Wow, when you put your mind to something, you really make it happen." However, every compliment was received with self-doubt. I was thinking, "If you knew the real me, you wouldn't feel that way or say that." Most people thought of me as an incredible person, mom, business leader and friend. But I knew it was a mask. My childhood was dark, and so were my secrets. I had always lived in fear, falsehood and forever worrying that I would be found out. There was so much shame in what had been done to me and what I had gone through. There was shame in who I was and some of the things I had done. Even though it may have been acting out of my trauma, I knew there were things I couldn't forgive about myself. But, to my credit, the intentional development of my mindset was what made me strong enough to confront my abuser, to leave toxic relationships, and to stand on my own two feet and financially as well. However, I didn't feel great or amazing. I was pretty messed up. As if the Universe wanted to provide evidence of that, I would only get so far and then the whole thing would collapse.

My 'perfect' marriage was a constant state of distrust, chaos, anger and hurt. Ever since he came back from Afghanistan, it felt was like he wasn't committed to us anymore. He was so different. Everything was different. I had held down the fort while he was gone . . . a new house, a new baby and working fulltime with a part-time business. Why wouldn't he come home at night? Was he having an affair?

I never should have asked him that. Now, we were really in a dark place. Sometimes he wouldn't say a word to me for days. If he did, another fight took place. I was crazy with anger and distrust. Why couldn't he see he was tearing us apart? Of course, to look at my Facebook page you would never know any of this. My feed was filled with thousands of likes and hearts of what others perceived to be an incredible union. Smile for the camera.

My body? Also, fake. The abs were real, but not the rest. The boobs certainly weren't. What was once easy to maintain, was now hard, and, for the first time meant depriving myself. Shame was my motivation. I hated those bumps on the back of my legs. I thought, "If I toned this up a bit more and didn't eat that, life would be better." I didn't feel healthy in my "fit"-ness. I had spent the better part of my adulthood coaching others on health and wellness, and I just wasn't healthy anymore. I was still wearing the mask.

Transformation arrived on an August day in the mountains.

The grass was cool and damp, but the air was hot and dry. Even at 8 AM and already approaching 80 degrees, I told myself, 'Just do it.' I was grateful that our rural life also meant that none of the neighbors could see me do this. No mask needed here. I opened my phone and on the YouTube app, pulled up the 'August 8th Lions Gate Meditation.' When this came across my feed, I had fallen on my knees in my kitchen in gut wrenching sadness. Now, I am sitting 'crisscross applesauce' (as my daughter would say) in my backyard hoping and praying, a meditation will change my life. I had never tried something like this before, but what the heck. What did I have to lose?

It is 8:08 am. I press play, close my eyes and turn my face towards the sun. It's warm, expanding light starts to melt into me. Suddenly there is a surge of energy. It's like the confluence of two raging rivers coming together in my chest. At first, I feel everything and everyone. I am not alone. We are all one and we are all connected. At the same time, I also feel my own essence, my uniqueness, my true self. I deserve to be here. No more judging, No more questioning. Suddenly I have a deep knowing. I am floating on the river of love and light and it's carrying me. I feel like I have come home, and someone has made warm chocolate chip cookies for me and the calories don't count. This home is my true home. It is Me . . . Authentic, true, divinely guided, loved and worthy me. The hot tears were streaming down my face as words start to come out of my mouth, "I deserve love. I am love. I will be love. I will show up as love. From now on only love exists." As I open my eyes, the world has come into sharper focus and is brighter.

I suddenly feel real and on purpose. The mask melts. The shame melts. Now there is only love. Deep Soul Self-love.

This is the best way to put into words the transformation I experienced in the grass that day. I'm not saying that from that moment on everything in my life has been perfect. I still have struggles and stress. I have missteps, mistakes, and misunderstandings. The hurricane of life continues, as it does for all of us, but now I turn inward, and my love becomes the eye of the storm that calms me. It reminds me who I am. I am divine. I am living my purpose just by being me.

You may ask, "Did things get better? Did everything change?" Yes, it did. My shift into unconditional love and authenticity has refined everything. Love was the missing link between the mind, body and soul connection. (The Divine Trine as I now call it). It shifted my marriage and how I see my husband. I was able to turn inward and see my own triggers from childhood that were causing me to act out in fear. Now I act out of love. I see how hard my husband was trying to provide for us, like the good man he is.

For me, I seek awareness when tripping over my trauma and try to react differently. I forgive myself and others and appreciate the learning. My ways of being a mother have shifted because I can create a loving, stable home environment and with a compassionate heart, guide my daughter. My friendships have shifted as I am now more authentic and share my history and feeling with them. They now KNOW me, the real me. My abundance has shifted because now instead of starting with goals on how to attain what is lacking, I start with a list of what I am grateful for that I already have. Then, I gratefully deserve more. Happy, thank you, more, please. The mindset matches the heart. My Facebook is for real; so is my smile. I have re-discovered some of my own unique and divinely given gifts.

I no longer resist or fear the unknown or changes that come my way. I know the Divine love is alive in me and I live with trust in the Divine plan. Now I simply ask," What's next?" with joyous expansion.

The Divine lives inside each and every one of us. I now live with a passion in helping others find it. We only need to turn inwards. We can all access that inner guru to guide us towards our true selves, our true purpose and our true unconditional love. ✿

Notes

TRANSFORMATION

Jackie Graybill

With a unique background in music, communication and the arts, Seattle, Nashville and London based transformational keynote speaker/singer/songwriter/podcaster and author Jackie Graybill inspires and transforms her audiences. Jackie has taught piano for the past 23 years, has lit up the stage in eight plays and musicals and placed in the Top 10 as Miss Puget Sound 2006 at Miss America's Miss Washington Pageant. She has released two albums and multiple singles to Spotify success (as Jackie Gray). She is also a Toastmasters International Speech Contest Winner for District 9 in 2021. Jackie's colorful life came crashing down into darkness when she found herself in an abusive marriage. Now free, and an overcomer who holds a Masters in Understanding Domestic and Sexual Violence, Jackie combines her original music with a message of hope by helping others recognize, escape and heal from abusive relationships.

Contact
Website: www.jackiegraybillspeaks.com
Email: booking.jackiespeaks@gmail.com

How My Abusive Marriage Gave Me An Unexpected Gift

By Jackie Graybill

"When I let go of what I am, I become what I might be."

— Lao Tzu

The sound of Clair de Lune drifted up the grand staircase at the Belmont Mansion and she looked down on her family and friends. The girl felt like the heroine in a fairytale, about to experience her happily-ever-after. Outside, deep snow blanketed the city of Nashville, a fairy wonderland effect that shaped her wedding in surprising ways.

The girl wasn't wearing her own wedding dress, as it was locked away in a dry cleaners' building, closed due to the inclement weather. Notable absences included three groomsmen, two flower girls, and multiple others. There had been no rehearsal or dinner the night before.

In spite of all this, her wedding day was one of the happiest she'd experienced, because of the hope and celebration it held. She was to marry the love of her life!

She descended the staircase barefoot, as her heels weren't the right height for the borrowed dress she was wearing. She caught sight of her fiance' and all nerves left her body, replaced by overwhelming love. She knew they would live happily-ever-after.

Except, they didn't.

We didn't.

Instead of beginning a life of love and joy, the hopeful girl I was, entered a dark time of constantly walking on eggshells, uncertain of what unpleasantness would come her way next, unsure of what had gone wrong and not knowing what she could do to fix it.

In time, the girl I was, would trade in her innocence, her bright shiny acceptance and love for every person on the planet, for strength, courage and fortitude.

She would walk a road paved in heartbreak, leading to an undeniable mission of helping other women escape, understand and heal from the abuse they've encountered. If I could, I would go back and tell the girl I was, that evolving would be painful, but that her butterfly wings would be worth it.

When I tell people I was in an abusive marriage, they conjure images of a punch to my face or hands around my throat. These weren't a part of my story, as they aren't for many other abuse survivors.

After I escaped my abusive marriage, I earned a Master's Degree in "Understanding Domestic and Sexual Violence." I learned that 40% of all adults have experienced an abusive relationship, and that physical abuse is just one of the many tools an abusive person utilizes to fulfill their main objective: maintaining power and control over their victim.

My ex-husband was collecting data on me for months before we were married. He knew my hopes and fears, my dreams and patterns, that I was loving, forgiving and positive. He knew I would be the first one to apologize after a fight, even if it wasn't my fault, because I hated conflict. He knew everything about me, and I could never have imagined that the traits I was proud of would be used against me.

It began slowly, with the undermining of my sanity I now know to be "gaslighting." He began training me to self-regulate when he wasn't there. I had to turn the lights off in any room before exiting to another, or he would chide me, saying, "the electricity costs money and you're wasting it!" Our combined to-do list became a battlefield because I "didn't do it right." We only ate out if we were able to use coupons. We grocery shopped together and only bought items that were on sale. He was beyond frugal. I wasn't allowed to buy anything for myself when we were together.

I had no idea that in 97% of abusive relationships, there is financial abuse. He really excelled in this area! I told myself he was stressed about money because he'd lost his job right before our wedding. Sixteen months later, he was still unemployed. Yet, he urged me to "get a job," because he didn't see my income as a piano teacher as bringing in enough, even though he had a rental property and we had a roommate (not ideal for newlyweds, but he insisted). Our finances were kept completely separate, and I was required to pay him half of the cost for essentials, while still taking care of my individual costs. It was a financial roommate situation, and he never let me forget the few times when I asked for his help to pay for my medical insurance.

He dictated what we ate, under the guise of his having our best health interests in mind. If I deviated from our gluten-free-pescatarian-non-dairy-low-salt-low-sugar diet, he called me a "splegan" (combining "splurge" and "vegan").

When he finally got a job, things got worse, and I realized our problems weren't mine alone.

He suggested we go to marriage counseling, probably thinking that he would have more to hang over my head, but the therapist saw through him, and suggested we see therapists individually. I had met my insurance deductible so I sought out a legitimate therapist. He began seeing a church intern with no experience (and the price tag of "free") who told him the problem was not with him, but with the marriage, and that we should return to couples counseling. Thankfully, our marriage therapist declined to treat us together.

I cried all the time and there were no good or happy areas in my life. My marriage was worse than terrible. Even though I'm a singer/songwriter (Jackie Gray is my stage name), which was why I moved to Nashville, I stopped writing music and left my band. I never saw my friends without him, and we left my church community to find one together, further isolating me. My three rocks during this time were my sister Jennifer, my Grandma, and my therapist, Alicia.

I remember the day Alicia recommended two books that would set off light bulbs in my brain. I started listening to *The Verbally Abusive Relationship: How to Recognize It and How To Respond* by Patricia Evans (on audiobook) as I drove out of the clinic parking lot. I was gobsmacked, my jaw hanging open as I drove, everything I was experiencing explained. Then I read *Why Does He Do That: Inside the Minds of Angry and Controlling Men* by Lundy Bancroft and the pieces began further falling into place.

I began looking at my interactions with my husband in an objective light, as if I were an outsider. He doesn't like boundaries. Check. He's unable to apologize. Check. He blames others and me for everything he doesn't like in his life. Check. He wants me to sell my car to further isolate me. Check. And on and on.

I shared my troubles with my grandma, then with my sister, then with friends. It turned out that each one had a piece of the "not sure about this guy" puzzle, but because they never compared notes, no one saw the whole picture or said anything to me.

I became more convinced than ever about what was happening and what I was experiencing. Then, I began praying for breadcrumbs to lead me in the right direction, either a future with him or an unknown future with me on my own. Those two possibilities were heavy to hold at the same time, but I did my best.

After reading another Patricia Evans book, *The Verbally Abusive Man: A Woman's Guide To Deciding Whether To Stay or Go*, I decided to follow her advice and present him with a copy of '*The Agreement.*' It included every abusive thing I could think of that he had said or done. We would both sign, and agree not to say or do any of those things to each other. His response would tell me everything I needed to know.

I began to read '*The Agreement*' aloud to him, but didn't get far, as he abruptly left and refused to speak to me. As he was heading to work the next morning, I mentioned that I left him a copy of '*The Agreement.*' His words were chilling, "You know, with that '*Agreement*,' it's like you're saying, "I don't like who I married. I want you to change who you are. Sign on the dotted line." I realized then, that he equated his personhood with his abusive words and actions, and it was time to leave. I packed a bag and moved out that very morning. I began attending an abuse support group and told him I would only consider moving back in if he completed a Batterers Intervention Class (the teacher would eventually kick him out because of his classroom behavior).

Then came the day that changed everything.

I was having dinner with a friend from out of town. My phone and location services were turned off, and we were at the back of the restaurant. There was no way my husband could know where I was, yet I looked up and was shocked to see him charging straight at me, yelling and making a scene! Thankfully, my friend never left my side, and my unhinged husband finally left.

That was the last time I saw him, except for the day our divorce finalized, nearly two years later. I eventually learned how he found me: a GPS tracker he hid in my car. I ended up living in a Domestic Violence Shelter for two months and cut off all contact with him. If he could do that in a restaurant, what else was he capable of doing? It wasn't worth finding out!

I was lucky. The average number of times an abuse victim tries to leave before they're finally successful is seven. I got out after one attempt and never went back. When I reflect on my past accomplishments, that's the one I'm most proud of and most grateful for.

This experience transformed me and changed the trajectory of my life.

I continued to heal and work with my therapist. As a fringe benefit, my longstanding fear of dogs dissipated! As my divorce dragged on, I became a dog mama for the first time. My little love is a teddy bear mini goldendoodle named Tyrion, after my favorite Game of Thrones character. Today, Tyrion is my best friend and trained PTSD service/assistance dog. He accompanies me everywhere and his love has helped heal me. I can't imagine my life without him!

After my divorce, I was still fearful of my ex-husband, and when my mother called me one day with a generous offer, I took her up on it. In December of 2019, I packed up my life in my beloved Nashville, and left all of my friends to move in with my parents in eastern Washington state.

Then, COVID happened.

It was the best place to wait out a pandemic, and COVID offered a lot of time to ponder my next steps. I couldn't get another city out of my mind. I had visited a friend in London just after my divorce and I fell in love with the city. I eventually found a Master's program in the UK that was a perfect fit: "Understanding Domestic and Sexual Violence."

In 2021, I graduated and Tyrion and I now live in incredible London!

After much healing work over the years, though I would never wish to go through my abusive marriage again, I'm finally grateful it happened. It brought me to London. It helped transform that naive, sweet and innocent girl I was, into a woman made of strength, grit and the knowledge that I can get through anything life throws at me. As long as I have my sweet little love, Tyrion, at my side, I am able to tackle any challenge.

The desire for a happily-ever-after has been replaced with a burning mission to help other women understand what they've experienced and heal from it. My hard-won journey and education, together with my supportive family and friends, have gifted me an incredible gem: the desire and tools to make a difference in the lives of others.

On the other side of the miles I've traversed, I wouldn't trade the journey for anything.

It has transformed me. ❁

Notes

 Wheeler

K DB (Karmen De Bora) Wheeler was not expecting a stroke to change the trajectory of her Executive and Leadership Coaching business at the beginning of 2021.

Her Seven Tools became strategies that helped her survive and transform her experience into a positive and successful outcome.

Encouraged by medical staff, colleagues, and friends, KDB used her vivid story-telling skills to rewrite the narrative of recovery. KDB has been coaching executives and leaders over the past decade.

Her unique certifications include George Washington University's Center for Excellence in Public Leadership e-Co Executive Leadership Coaching, Barrett Values® Centre Certified CT Consultant and Leadership Embodiment® certifications, the University of Santa Monica's LM&SCL Il certification. She is an International Coach Federation® certified PCC coach. KDB graduated *magna cum laude* from National-Louis University with a Bachelor of Science in Management.

Contact

Email: 7Tools.kdbw@gmail.com

I Wonder if I'm Having a Stroke

By KDB (Karmen De Bora) Wheeler

"You may encounter many defeats, but you must not be defeated. In fact, it may be necessary to encounter the defeats, so you can know who you are, what you can rise from, how you can still come out of it. "

– Maya Angelou

It's surreal to realize that eight simple words define the life-changing event when a blood vessel bursts in your brain. Welcome to the beginning of your new normal.

Time slows as you watch your own body falling to the floor. This out-of-body experience is punctuated when your brain registers, "I'm wedged between my furniture." The left side of your body hits the ground first, and the remaining auto responses you possess send a command to your right hand, "Grab your mobile phone". Trying to grasp the phone from this angle looks like a scene from the medical drama series Transplant. Your attempt to use the phone only confirms the worst; yes, you are having a stroke.

The gravity of your circumstances weighs heavier on you with each moment. Fire Department Emergency Medical Technicians are breaking through the door. Everyone is speaking forcefully, nearly shouting as you are hoisted up off the floor onto a stretcher. The ambulance is rushing you to the hospital, with requisite sirens blaring. The emergency room professionals scramble to administer TPA medication to help restore blood flow to your brain in hopes of preventing severe stroke damage. Even through semi-consciousness, you hear everything as if you're a bystander in the next room. Did we get here fast enough? Will the medication work? Among the terrifying thoughts racing through my mind was, "And if this doesn't work, what will?"

It doesn't matter the size of the blood vessel that bursts – where or on which side of your brain it happened – your life will be impacted; routines will be disrupted. Comprehension, speech, mobility, strength, and dexterity all become distant goals in the long process of relearning, and, just for clarification, I was one of the lucky ones.

I was lucky enough to arrive at the emergency room within the critical three-hour window for the administration of the TPA medication to be effective . . . lucky enough to be recovering at home within three months. And I was lucky enough to be here to share my story and the seven tools that helped me achieve my recovery goals.

These seven tools are just a few of the tools I have mastered over my years. And these seven, in particular, are what became the foundation and pillars of my successful recovery. They also kept me from spiraling down into despair and reminded me of my life's purpose.

It started when I had regained enough consciousness in the hospital's Intensive Care Unit. *Affirmations* and expressing daily *Gratitude* helped me view my new reality with a more positive outlook. When the initial horror of being paralyzed on my left side felt like too much to digest, I was relieved and very grateful to learn that the paralysis was expected to be temporary – as in, it might take a year to resolve versus being permanent. I expressed my primary affirmation mantra, "I am so happy and grateful now that I have full use of the left side of my body" on a daily basis. Other affirmations were added as the weeks and months progressed.

Thankfully, the part of my brain where my comedic slant on life is stored was fully intact! I relied on humor to fuel hope in my recovery and anchor my sanity. *Monty Python's Flying Circus* captured it perfectly in one of their most remembered skits, "NO-body expects the Spanish Inquisition!" This seemed more than apropos of my situation. Trust me, a blood vessel bursting in my brain was not on my list of expected plans for 2021 – not even a footnote.

My plans were now being determined by the hospital's rehabilitation unit's Stroke Recovery Strategies, and my first goal was set – to leave Acute Rehabilitation walking. That goal was quickly superseded when the doctors informed me that use of my left side would only return through intense therapies – therapy in multiple forms, in multiple stages, and over time. My focus on leaving this unit walking in heels was far-fetched. As I remember this formidable goal, all I can say is, "Seriously, heels?!"

My imagination of Inpatient Rehabilitation and home recovery was an illusion of leisure and idealism. Here is what I thought I would find in an average day's schedule: sleeping in, undemanding breakfasts, and some therapy here and there; a welcomed light lunch, a timely nap, maybe a little more therapy. Why not add a proper cocktail hour, culminating in a replenishing dinner? I imagined days accented with the occasional scintillating medical conversation with technicians, nurses, and doctors. What utopian hospital scene did I float in from?

My recovery made me feel as if I were in a time warp. The process of regaining use of my left side required creativity and determination. Imagine a fish that you toss onto the shore that is desperately trying to make it back to the river. There was a lot of flailing! With that fish in mind, I started to think of the next goal I would eventually add to the list – cooking. I could not begin to imagine cooking in my current physical state.

Suddenly, my recovery goals seemed to compound and feel insurmountable.

Reframing gave me the power to flip my script and rewrite a new story that would move me more closely to the reality I wanted – one where I was using my left hand, arm, leg, and foot. Incremental goals would be critical to keep my recovery momentum going, as well as support my psychological and emotional well-being. All my daily activities, such as shopping, cooking, cleaning, and more, would require learning new strategies; but first, we had to get the left arm and hand to wake up. Reframing allowed me to adjust my perspective on the long road to recovery and focus on the small step goals. Reframing also provided a tool to flip the negative medical information into more positive mental and emotional frameworks for me.

It was self-compassion and self-forgiveness that staved off feelings of inadequacy. In fairness, this was the first time I had ever experienced my body not responding to brain signals for movement. *Compassion and Forgiveness* allowed me to recognize that I am only human. I am not invincible.

I allowed myself to be self-compassionate by becoming my own best friend and being kind. I turned to self-forgiveness any time my mind wandered into the deep, dark woods where I placed blame on myself for even having a stroke. Being able to release these types of feelings helped me to promote a better sense of well-being. I forgave myself and, in doing so, allowed my body, mind, and spirit to begin to heal.

It was an example from an Occupational Therapist that really invoked my empathy and self-compassion. She explained that the area of the brain that sends signals to your arm is like an expressway. The stroke created the need for infrastructure repairs. During these repairs, traffic (aka neurological signals) was being detoured. Eventually, the expressway would be repaired and reopened, allowing the brain to send signals to my arm again. Recovery was within reach, and yet there were still challenges ahead for me to overcome.

With this new frame of reference, my focus never wavered from daily goals using other tools that were familiar and reliable such as meditation and centering.

Meditation was how I chose to start and end each day. It was also the response I chose when feeling anxious, terrified, or apprehensive. Meditation was not a new practice for me. As I've said, these tools are ones that were commonplace in my life. I had already realized many of the benefits that could be achieved by incorporating meditation into my daily habits.

Centering quieted the mental chatter, dialed down emotional fears, and created a state of internal calm. This quickly became my "go-to" tool when relearning to walk. The breathing part of it was especially helpful. One of the many frustrating exercises I did daily was figuring out how to get my left foot to remember it was connected to my leg. Even my left knee and hip were "disconnected". The worst of the disconnected neurological wiring was the part of my brain that kept me balanced.

The medical staff nicknamed me the "Therapy Warrior." They cheered me on with my laser-focused determination. While they laughed at my humor, it was the one constant and simple tool in my toolbox, that found its purpose throughout every day of my Inpatient Rehabilitation recovery.

It is no secret that music is an effective form of therapy. I took advantage of an already established habit to further my success in recovery. *Music* was a natural, yet essential tool during this time. *"My Life with a Soundtrack." A smile appears across your face as you are wrapped in benevolent beats. Your brain feels focused, yet calm. A sense of peace washes over you as a blend of harmonies fill the space around you.*

My gratitude is overflowing today as I reflect on the amazing individuals and care I received throughout this time. I continue to express my gratitude with everyone I encounter. My family and friends were/are invaluable in my recovery.

My recovery path has been paved by these life-affirming processes and practices that I now call *The 7 Most Important Tools for Bouncing Back from Any Traumatic Experience.*

Here is a recap of all seven tools, along with a brief description of each.

1. **Affirmations & Gratitude:** Gratitude comes from the Latin word gratus, meaning "pleasing, thankful". Both of these tools promote thoughts and feelings of appreciation and have similar positive responses. They train the mind and emotions to disconnect and shift into a different orientation to your situation. They both actively promote a self-empowerment perspective through these types of declarations.

2. **Humor:** Humor is all about the quality of being amusing, as well as being a mood or state of mind. It is able to take a more

light-hearted view of the circumstances. There are multiple applications with humor that have the capability to seismically change, modify, and shift your moods and perspectives.

3. **Reframing:** This tool is about the practice of assessing a situation, thought, or feeling from another point of view. It provides a framework – literally – to positively reprogram your brain. It is about rewriting the story you are currently telling yourself.

4. **Compassion & Forgiveness:** Self-compassion is about being your own best friend by extending kindness to yourself, especially in instances of perceived inadequacy. Self-forgiveness allows you to focus your decisions to release any feelings of resentment or vengeance towards yourself.

5. **Meditation:** Meditation is a technique designed with the intention to encourage one's heightened state of both awareness and focused attention. This is a widely known consciousness-changing practice. Medical studies show it to have a range of benefits on psychological, emotional, and physical well-being.

6. **Centering:** This technique is widely practiced in the martial arts Aikido and Kung Fu. This practice is known for ensuring you remain grounded, calm, and relaxed, especially in stressful situations. It also utilizes better breathing to maintain a clear mind.

7. **Music:** While Music Therapy has been used for years, there are now new domains in neuroscience studies. Used in various forms, it is valued for encouraging you to smile. It can lift your spirits, focus your brain, and calm your senses. Research suggests movement (i.e., dancing, exercising) to music also boosts endorphins – the "feel good" messengers in our bodies.

All of these practices, combined, have saved my life – from sanity to well-being. I now teach them to others. It is always immensely gratifying to hear success stories from my clients through their use of one or many of these tools.

It is my wish, should you ever find yourself seeking ways to refocus, adjust and/or renew your spirits after a traumatic experience, that these tools will help you, too – with your recovery.

Hey, I'll even throw in "*How to Create Your Own Life with a Soundtrack.*" – no rehabilitation required. ❁

Notes

Addy Kujawa

Addy Kujawa, CAE, DES, is a Jack Canfield Success Principles® Certified Transformation Trainer, Certified Association Executive, certified Digital Event Strategist, author, and international speaker. She is CEO for AAOE and The Radical Change Group, the latter founded with her husband in the middle of Covid in the spirit of beginning something to serve others in a big and meaningful way.

In her chapter, Addy shares her personal story of transforming her relationship with her mom. It is a journey of moving away from feeling alone and forgotten to a place of feeling held up and truly supported.

She is wife to her fabulous, supportive husband, Kermit, mom to her two beautiful, and incredibly amazing children, Xavier and Sophie, and though they are in college, host mom to Peter and Steven, two sweet and absolutely wonderful young men.

Contact

Website: radicalchangegroup.com
Email: addykujawa@theradicalchangegroup.com

From Gritted Teeth to Deep Conversation

By Addy Kujawa

"Love and caring can take strange forms before you understand fully."

— Anonymous

I believed that it was too late to have the relationship with my mom that I had always dreamed of having. We had fights, felt judged and criticized by each other, and felt a long, long way apart. I would sometimes go weeks or months before the guilt would build to a crescendo and I would finally call her, gritting my teeth.

Through working on myself, I discovered a path through the negative stories we were both carrying to a relationship filled with love, encouragement, and support.

Gritting My Teeth

As I sat in the front row at the junior high Forensics competition, I was reviewing my memorized story that I needed to tell everyone. I'd practiced so hard and I knew it front to back. I was excited, nervous, and ready to get my turn. The judge, sitting at the back of the room at the teacher's desk, called the first student. She walked to the front of the room, turned, and launched into her story. I was shocked. It was my story. MY story. How could she be telling the same story? I had no idea that might happen, and I was thrown for a loop. Panicked. She was doing an amazing job.

How could I do the same story? I'll look like I'm copying her. There's nothing I can do. I'm rooted to my chair, sweating like I'm at the lake on a 90-degree summer day with the sun beating down on me. Suddenly she was walking back to her seat, and I hadn't heard a word. The judge called the next contestant. It was me. ME?! Oh no. No, no, no. My head snapped back to double check. He said my name again. I stood and my legs almost gave out. I walked slowly to the front of the room and turned around. I took a deep breath to start. And I took another deep breath. The entire story had left my brain. It was as if I had never read it, much less practiced it.

What do I do? My face flushed, and I could feel that deep redness on my pale face bloom. My eyes darted to the judge and he was sitting back, arms crossed, brow furrowed, and a full frown on his face. I stared at the girl silently pleading for her to cast me the first line. Please. The first word. Anything at all. She leaned back in her chair and smiled. I began to sob and returned to my seat. The competition continued.

At the end, I sat with my head bowed waiting for everyone else to leave first, deeply aware that I was on my own. A mom approached me and put her hand on my back and asked if I was ok. I realized it was the mom of the girl that did so well with "my" story. I nodded and said I was fine.

I had a long walk home by myself before I needed to break the news that I had failed. Utterly.

I was a senior in high school, standing on the block at an "away" swim meet. I was the last leg of a relay where we were in last place. Last place meaning by the time I jumped in the water, all the other lanes had finished. I was beat red knowing I was not the strongest swimmer and the entire room would be watching me swim four laps completely by myself. The only good thing about swimming competition is that you can cry and no one can tell. You had to "lose" your goggles of course, and you had to be careful about your breathing, but those tears could fall and be swept away by the over-chlorinated water, never to be seen or noticed. I closed my eyes on every breath so I couldn't see anything. I finally reached the end and dragged myself up and out of the pool. Someone else's mom was there with a towel, a loving embrace, and words of comfort.

I didn't have any parents in the stands this time either.

My parents were visiting, and I was wondering why I put myself through this again. Judgment, criticism, and what I was doing wrong felt like the only viable topics for a conversation. According to my parents, I was living my life all wrong, parenting wrong, working my job wrong, and even being in a relationship wrong. "Why don't I just" was a favorite conversation starter. And somehow, even talking about books or movies or holidays created a path to these three topics. I even gave up the master bedroom to my parents to catch a break. A compliment? Something I was doing well, or right? That never seemed to happen. I finally couldn't take it anymore. I was fed up. I escaped to dry my wet hair in the extra bathroom at the top of the stairs. I turned on the blow dryer and I was fuming. I said all the things I wanted to say to my mom in the privacy of the bathroom. I was going on and on because I was angry, and I was done. And then I heard my mom shout up the stairs, "It's only loud to YOU Ad!" They heard my ranting and raving and then I couldn't even be mad anymore. I was absolutely mortified. I didn't want to make them feel bad. UGH! I had to apologize and grovel.

I had a million of these stories. My mom wasn't there. My mom didn't love me. My mom didn't care. They felt like chains around my neck and waist keeping me from living. They kept me from being and existing in real time.

My Work

I'm at a Tony Robbins Motivational Speaking event, and he is guiding us through an exercise, which is a meditation of a past event. I remembered a time when I was four or five and I was searching for my Easter basket. I couldn't find it. It was a favorite story my parents told because they said that all I kept doing was wandering in a circle saying, "I can't find it." It was hilarious in their eyes. I hated that story. It felt embarrassing and cruel.

Tony had to drudge it up again. He had us watch from above as if we were other people in the room and think what they're thinking and feel what they're feeling. And when I pretended that I was my parents, I was laughing. It was pretty funny. An adorable little girl wandering in a little circle expecting her basket to either call out her name or appear right in front of her. And when the meditation was over, I was filled with affection knowing that my parents loved me and cared for me and saw for the first time the humor in that situation. I also knew that I didn't have to search long – it was under the piano bench – which is what really makes the story more entertaining. When I could see it from their perspective, it changed mine.

I was in a Jack Canfield class and learning about *The Success Principles*. Something he said struck me in the heart, and I have to rewind the program to hear it again. He said again, "It's important to understand that everyone is doing the best they can in any moment, with the tools and resources and skills they have." My first thought was 'No, they aren't.' Then I thought *'Am I doing the best I can in any given situation with the tools and resources and skills I've learned?'*

I realized that yes, in fact, I have always been a lifelong learner, and I feel like it's been a hard road to dig out of my childhood. I learned how to not lash out or cut people out of my life without explanation. I learned not to hide under the covers because I couldn't deal with the world for a few days. I would like people to know that I'm doing the best I can in any given moment because I really am. That doesn't mean I live perfectly. It does mean that I'm constantly growing and evolving and my responses reflect that. And, I am giving my parents, mainly my mom, that grace. Can I believe she was always doing the best she could? Can I change my perspective of my mom? I would like to think so.

Suddenly I'm flooded with more memories. I remembered days at the lake and weeks at my grandparents' cabin. There were Valentines' Days and St. Patrick's Days with small gifts and special meals. A call. A hug. A card. An unexpected gift. Thoughtful Christmas events and picnics at many parks. Times with my family. Times with my parents. Times with my mom.

The Visits

We carefully planned a trip to visit my family and worked to avoid creating any of the painful memories of past gatherings. We got our own place. We budgeted meals we could cook and meals we could treat them to as well. We thought of ways we could give back to my parents and we decided to see their pictures and talk about all the adventures. We brought games and promised ourselves that we could have the mornings and evenings to our own little family. We went wanting to give rather than take. We went wanting to share love and light rather than get what's coming to us. The plan was a success all the way around. We've never had such fun or enjoyed each other so much. We've had good times, but this is a whole other level. This is what I had always dreamed of having with my parents.

I asked them to visit us. We would host them in our house. I was nervous and worried, and there was no escape once they had agreed! We made plans and we made dinner together and kept it very low key. I did this purposely rather than trying to prove myself in every possible way that I was good enough. We went shopping at the new Ikea and my mom and I spent hours wandering around while our husbands checked out the café. We talked and looked at everything. It was the most connected and loving experience I ever felt with my mom.

We watched movies and napped and when they left, I didn't cry.

It was the first time I hadn't cried when they departed in decades. I wondered why? I realized that I thought I used to cry to show my mom I cared – that I loved her and would miss her. Maybe I even cried a little bit out of guilt for how I treated her. But I didn't feel the need to cry this time because I didn't need the last-ditch effort to prove I cared.

I realized later that this was the first time we had spent a visit together where I showed her how much I loved her and where she showed me how much she loved and accepted me. She listened, celebrated and encouraged me.

Realization

I called her a couple of weeks ago and asked her if she remembered the hair dryer story. She didn't. So, I told her, and we laughed so hard together. That's the relationship I always dreamed of having with her. And I didn't create it by myself. My mom wanted it too. It just took me a long time to realize that. ✸

Notes

Karen Durham

K aren's career spans 30 years, primarily in Mental Health Nursing, in addition to Success Coaching. There were no barriers she allowed to hinder her. From single parenting, being advised she needed a master's degree to advance her career, to overcoming with God's grace, sudden, critical health challenges, she faced them all with courage and tenacity.

Karen is a self-proclaimed lover of Christ, life, family, learning and classical (among other genres) music. She is a daughter, sister, mother, and gran pup mom of one.

Apart from the loves, she is a creative who can be found behind a camera and cooking/baking, developing, testing, and adjusting recipes to complement her vegetarian lifestyle (friends and family are the beneficiaries of such). She also enjoys nature and walking. She is a trained guide for Strala Yoga.

Her latest endeavor is to coach women over 45 years desiring transformation as she is a living model for that.

Bermuda is her home, the world her oyster.

Contact

Website: www.karenmdurham.bm

My Transformation aka Cinderella Story

By Karen Durham

*"Having courage does not mean that we are unafraid.
Having courage and showing courage means we face our fears.
We are able to say, 'I have fallen, but I will get up.'"*

— Maya Angelo

B e that person . . . who makes a difference in the lives of others. I recall that 'Happy Monday', February 6, 2006, being at work when everything quickly turned 'south'. That was the last day I would spend on my home island, Bermuda, for three months.

I'm getting ahead of myself, I should start from the beginning.

Take two!

Once upon a time, as the fairy tale goes, yours truly was Cinderella for one interminable day. Minus the ball. Minus the glass slipper. Minus the prince.

Always being one to seek the positives:

I had my own carriage (aka Air Ambulance) that flew me from my home in Bermuda to Boston, Massachusetts, USA and contrary to Cinderella's timing – long after midnight!

I arrived adorned in the prized ballroom attire, hospital gown, a popular designer whose name remains unknown today, however, that was the least of my concerns.

My first carriage: A colleague's car.

My ballroom: The Emergency Room.

My attendants: ER medical staff, family, friends and most importantly GOD!

The prior week, on 'Friyay' January 29, 2006, standing on a hill, finalizing transportation plans with a colleague to visit clients, I was suddenly assaulted by the car door to which I was standing near. One witness. No sirens. A self-assessment which proved no visual injury.

Therefore, life proceeded as usual.

Fast forward to the 'Happy Monday' previously referred to, after arriving at work 30 minutes early, I was never early to work, which should have been an indication something was severely off. I was plagued with the most torturous headache imaginable.

This was the start of my Cinderella story.

During those first challenging days with 24-hr monitoring, numerous blood tests, sedation, and trepidation, my angel mom was by my side from the start. Other family members soon traveled to Boston to support me.

My faith and that of my family's rested in God's healing power and sustained me during the acute phase of that sudden illness. After a few weeks, I was chosen for a second carriage ride to a rehab hospital! The days were long and the following friends and support team were giants in my recovery:

RNs

Physicians

Physiotherapist

Occupational therapist

Speech and language therapist

Dietician

Psychologist

Social Workers

And the nights were equally long plus 'entertaining'. I was the 'audience of one' with my roommate perfecting her acoustics nightly, that evidently kept me awake. This was not Physician Ordered.

Determination and persistence were imperative; from asking for and being granted 'full time status' where additional therapy sessions were given from 9 am – 4 pm weekdays. They were emotionally and psychologically draining, but I had a goal to achieve. My goal was to recover and support my 13-year-old daughter again. I was the single parent and I had to recover for her. She was (and still is) my WHY!

So being asked by a psychologist to consider returning to employ-ment as a non-professional because I did not perform adequately to the anticipated level in the test, further fueled my determination. My family suggested that the test administrator find additional assessments to reconsider the findings. I was constantly reminded of the famous Bible verse an aunt wrote in every card she gave me, Proverbs 3:5-6: *'Trust in the Lord with all your heart and lean not on your own understanding; in all your ways submit to him, and he will make your paths straight.'*

I am eternally grateful for her support with those words which I was able to reflect upon and practice.

I lived a dream life – residing abroad for months, various family visiting, living as a tourist with all expenses paid. But, everything in life has a cost and this dream was at the expense of my physical and mental health. On the other hand, it's said 'not to be sorry (for your) experiences as we learn from them and can use the wisdom to help others along their journey.'

I returned home to Bermuda continuing therapy, but less intense. I was exhausted and had challenges in so many areas of life that I moved in with my parents. The Bible verse continuously played – TRUST and SUBMIT to God and those who supported me.

I was at what seemed to be near the end of my rehabilitation road. Trust was all I was able to do.

Then came the 'reveal' day after what seemed an eternity, actually seven months, I was able to wear Cinderella's slipper and walk, run, drive, and begin part-time employment. I could see the light at the end of the tunnel.

When employed in an area I detested, a close friend reminded me to be grateful. That forced me to look extensively at what I had overcome. Medically, I had defeated two major health obstacles. After twelve months without full time employment my financial commitments were current.

Then four months from that awakening, after much prayer and a changed attitude, I interviewed and was employed as a Nurse Supervisor. Remembering the psychologist's initial prediction that I would not be capable of returning to professional employment, I felt accomplished.

God always has the final say! The hidden treasure was the acoustic neuroma (benign ear tumor) discovered during the ER visit on my Cinderella night. The treatment of the sudden illness prioritized over the resection of the tumor. There were five years of bi-annual monitoring of the growth and effects of the ear tumor. That was until the surgeon, astonished that I was not experiencing more negative effects predicted that I would need surgery. The dreaded extended medical leave was positive this time because I could 'plan' for it and earn while on leave.

Cinderella repeated herself. Back to Boston. Family support. Intensive and extensive medical care. Lengthy rehab.

Philippians 4:6-7 reminds us *'Do not be anxious about anything, but in every situation, by prayer and petition, with thanksgiving, present your request to God. And the peace of God with transcends all understanding, will guard your hearts and your minds in Christ Jesus.'*

I no longer live the fairy tale life. I'm grateful for my health that I previously took for granted. My WHY (daughter) stands with me. My angel (mom) rejoices with God's angels as of August 2021.

I have found my purpose . . . Share my story to encourage and support other women to know TRANSFORMATION is achievable, as Matthew 19:26 says *'With God all things are possible.'*

"We delight in the beauty of the butterfly, but rarely admit the changes it has gone through to achieve that beauty." —Maya Angelo

"Stepping onto a brand-new path is difficult, but not more that remaining in a situation, which is not nurturing to the whole woman."
— Maya Angelo

Notes

Sue London

Sue London was faced with abuse, disease, divorce, near death, and a life and death pregnancy. She soared above these challenges with the help of a furry friend named Rocky. Now Sue has transformed her life and is a successful Media Presence, Pet Psychic, Reiki Master and Intuitive Life Coach. Sue proudly shares that it has been a true honor to have helped thousands of people more deeply connect with their own true self and with that of their animals, both living and crossed over.

The messages she's been able to channel through the hearts and souls of pets have helped to heal relationships, provide closure, peace and understanding that might never have been possible without this empathic bridge. Sue is a firm believer that everything does happen in our life for a reason. The experiences she faced has made her a new and better person who really understands what others are going through.

Contact
Website: www.asksuelondon.ca
Email: sue@asksuelondon.ca

My Pets Transformed My Life

By Sue London

"Animals ease our pain, give us unconditional love, inspire courage and strength for us to transform our lives."

— Sue London

Spot, Rocky, and Molly saved my life! Pets communicate with us when we listen. I was three years old when we rescued Spot. Driving to the local Humane Society, my mother was adamant we were coming home with a non-shedding breed, preferably a poodle. I was drawn to the scared, undernourished shy terrier who was all white except for the brown spot on her back end. She sat in the cage all the way at the end of the room. This dog was a shedder!

Years later, I learned that Spot was scheduled to be put down later that day. I just knew we were meant to be together. Her eyes showed me that same sadness I felt within. We both had been abused in our lives. We completely understood each other. Spot had been dumped out of a moving car on the highway. As a result, car rides made her extremely nervous.

As a young sensitive child, I knew that it was my job to help her feel safe. Spot did everything in her power to protect me. It was as if she knew I was a lonely, abused only child. She sensed what I needed as I did for her. She listened when I shared my fears, my hopes, and my dreams. Many days and nights she licked my tears away. She slept alongside me in my bed with her body against my leg. Spot reminded me I was never alone.

As I got older and dated, Spot pointed out the nice boys and those that were not good for me. She attempted to warn me about my ex-husband not being right for me by growling and biting at his ankles. Interestingly she only bit him! At that time in my life, I didn't listen. Trust your pets! They sense our needs and know what to do to help and to protect us from those negative energies and those people who are not good for our well-being.

To this day, if I am hiring someone in person, my dogs are right there – wagging their tails with approval or growling with disapproval. Spot and I had nineteen wonderful years together, and she was the sibling I never had. Spot was even going to walk with me down the aisle. Four months before my wedding she got sick. My mother took her to the veterinary hospital, or so I was told. I learned two weeks later my mother had actually put Spot down without telling me. A friend shared the news with me. It broke my heart.

Seven years after I lost Spot I was asked by a concerned neighbor and friend to help him by giving Rocky, a one-year-old shih-tzu, a home. Now married to the man Spot tried to warn me about, I had to convince him that we needed to adopt Rocky. Rocky was going to be put down simply because he didn't have a home. When I first laid eyes on Rocky, I immediately picked him up. He put his head on my shoulder and placed his paws around my neck as if he were giving me a hug. He was dirty and badly in need of a haircut, but his eyes told it all. At the time, I had no idea how much he would mean to me. When we rescued Rocky from being put down, I couldn't imagine how he would save my life many times over.

Rescuing Rocky months earlier helped me through my first difficult pregnancy. This would be the first significant challenge in my life. In the seventh month of my pregnancy, I started having complications. The baby wanted to come earlier than expected. To prevent this from happening, my doctor ordered me to have complete bed rest. Rocky was there with me every step of the way. When I got frustrated or lonely, Rocky would somehow remind me that I was not alone. He would constantly lick me and look into my eyes. I sensed he was trying to tell me all would be okay.

In March 1988, I delivered a wonderful baby girl. When we brought Lynn home from the hospital Rocky never left her side. When she was three years old, she had vomited while sleeping on her back and had stopped breathing. Rocky alerted me by barking with great urgency. When I ran into Lynn's bedroom all my first aid training as a child came flooding back to me and I was able to clear the blockage and bring her back by giving her mouth-to-mouth resuscitation. Not only did Rocky communicate when Lynn was in danger, but that day I felt confidence come over me that maybe there were things in life that I did know. At that time, I had a father and husband telling me otherwise.

Pets help us heal. Months after Lynn was born, I began to quickly lose a lot of weight. Soon after I was diagnosed with Crohn's disease. This came as a huge blow. I was depressed, devastated and I wanted to give up. Once again, Rocky was there for me. I would spend hours at a time in the washroom vomiting and having diarrhea. Every time Rocky would scurry to be there with me before I shut the door. Our bathroom had turned into a play area for my little one. While I was sick, Rocky would entertain Lynn and keep her out of trouble. He would sit and lick my legs, cry, and sense the pain that I felt. It was so comforting to have him there beside me. I found him to be therapeutic. When I was in bed and experiencing the severe pain that can accompany Crohn's Disease, Rocky would move toward me, and breathe very heavily into my ear. It was as if he wanted me to focus on his breathing and not my pain. His presence taught me that by breathing deeply, I could handle the pain better.

In 1996, we had moved into a new house, my marriage was stressful, and I could not understand why my husband was never around. It was a horrible time. I started having strange feelings within my abdomen unlike anything I had ever experienced before. The doctor diagnosed it as a torn muscle. It made sense from all the gardening and stripping wallpaper that I had been doing in our new house, so I did not question the diagnosis. Hours later, my health worsened. I could not breathe, and the pain was excruciating. I was rushed to the hospital. I was told my intestine had burst and I had 30 minutes to live. All I could think about was what was going to happen to my dog. Seconds later, I was hovering over my body. I felt less pain. I watched doctors and nurses stressing around me, trying everything to bring me back. My attention turned to a tunnel that I began to go through, and then I came to a white light. In this white light I felt tremendous love, peace, and joy. These feelings were foreign to me, and I decided I wanted to stay. No longer did I finish that thought when two images stepped forward. It was my Grandpa Buck and Jesus. They shared with me it was not my time to join them. I needed to go back. My destiny was to help millions of people and animals cope, heal and move forward in their lives. Because I trusted these two beings, I came back, and life has never been the same.

When I was in the hospital recovering and building my strength again, I would visualize holding Rocky and him licking, cuddling, and giving me pet therapy. When I came home Rocky would nudge me to get me moving so I could continue to build my strength. He encouraged me to spend time in nature.

Pets give us strength and courage. Five years after Lynn was born, and Crohn's disease was in remission, I was pregnant with another child. Because I had Crohn's Disease, this became a high-risk pregnancy. I spent a few months in the hospital fighting to stay alive. Crohn's disease had flared up and my weight was down to eighty pounds. The doctor told me I had to make a choice. My choice was to decide who would live – me or my unborn baby. I knew I was pregnant for a reason and I was staying pregnant, and I knew we would both survive.

I fired my doctor!

The new doctor prescribed a visit from Rocky. At that time, pets were not allowed in hospitals. The next day the nurse came into my room and said she was going to get a wheelchair for me to see my best friend. At that point I could not walk four feet to the washroom. Knowing that my best friend was nearby, I found the strength and walked down the hall and out onto the patio. As I reached the patio doors Rocky was jumping up and down and wagging his tail with excitement. Instantly I started to cry. It was wonderful to see him. It was not long after that visit that I recovered and was on my way home again. Months later I delivered a beautiful healthy baby girl named Marie. The strength, courage, and determination Rocky gave to me was priceless.

In 1997, I learned the reasons why my husband never visited me when my intestine had burst, nor why he wasn't around much when the babies were born. My husband was having an affair, and I decided to end our 16-year marriage. After the near-death experience, I knew God had bigger plans for me and I simply didn't have to accept this man's abuse any longer. Rocky became my rock! When things were incredibly stressful, my 4-legged friend would be right there licking me and giving me love. He never left my side. That was his way of saying all would be okay. He was right. Many people would say to me, "You are going through all of this for a reason." Years later I can see that, but at the time I didn't believe them.

Five years later while working on my personal transformation, Ross came into my life, and Rocky's health started to fail. Ross was at my side when Rocky took his last breath. Rocky had found his replacement and knew I would be okay. Our other dog, Molly, who had been previously abused by a man, would usually cower down and pee. However, when Molly was around Ross, she would wag her tail and let him pick her up. When Marie met Ross, she noticed Molly's accepting behavior and said, "Mommy you have to marry this man!"

I did! Ross loves animals as much as I do.

Every step of my journey to transformation, pets on this side, and those crossed over have supported, encouraged, and loved me to never give up. They want me to grow to new heights and to continue to make a positive difference in our world for pets and their owners.

My pets helped me overcome abuse, disease, divorce, near death and a life and death pregnancy. They eased my pain, gave me unconditional love and the strength and courage to keep going.

They transformed my life!

Please consider sharing and receiving love with animals, I guarantee that it can be transformational and healing for you too. ✹

Jane Williams

Jane Williams is an Intuitive Energy Coach & Performing Arts Educator who helps people break through blocks to become the most abundant and best version of themselves. As a graduate of Michigan State University, Virginia Tech and The Dell'Arte School of Physical Theatre, Jane has worked in the performing arts and creativity field all her life. Jane is a Dow Creativity Fellow from Northwood University in Michigan and an Emerging Artist Recipient from the Durham Arts Council.

She has completed Jack Canfield's & Kathleen Seeley's Success Principles Virtual Skills Bootcamp; is on her RIM journey with Dr. Deb Sandella and is a Certified Barrett Values Centre Leadership & Coaching Consultant. Often referred to as "The Intuitive Archeologist," Jane continually looks for the best in people and how to unravel the "puzzle" of who they are and wish to become. She is honored and excited to be included in this book with her beautiful and transforming co-authors!

Contact
Website: www.janeawilliams.com
Email: jane@janeawilliams.com

Simply Profound Transformation

By Jane Williams

"Transformation isn't about adding more work to your life;
it is about shifting your perspective,
so life becomes more fun, magical and joyful."

— Sheri Salata

Louie, my tuxedo 'furline' and I watched a cardinal this morning. Louie alerted first; I followed as it is always so much fun to see life through his eyes and excitement. The cardinal, in his feathers he has changed to match his female, came to the birdbath on the outside deck to have just a sip of water at first. Before long, he had hopped into the bath and after an initial, splash in and out to keep an eye out for big, scary things, he began splashing with abandon. Sipping and splashing; sipping and splashing for just a moment in time. Louie never gave chase but was alert the entire time watching through the deck windows as was I looking through Louie's eyes. I watched a cardinal sipping and splashing this morning with one of my favorite beings in the whole wide world.

I was transformed.

One time I was driving through Montana, one of the biggest states

I have ever driven through. I had seriously misjudged my map and my time as usual, and at the end of a very long day of driving in a car WITHOUT air conditioning OR cruise control, I became grumpy and tired and defeated. It was still a loooooong way to where I was to stop for the night to rest and eat. I was sticky and grimy from driving with the windows closed now because of a sudden downpour of rain 'Great. Just GREAT. I'm sticky, far from my destination and hungry to boot.'

Not stopping but keeping on driving, I kept thinking about what was before me. While driving, as I usually do with most things in my life, I kept my eyes and thoughts on the future. 'Get there. Get THERE. GET THERE.' I was grumping and whining about how hot and icky I felt. In the middle of my tirade, I just happened to glance back in my rearview mirror.

The sight that greeted me was nothing short of holy. I was allowed to view one of the most stunning sunsets I had and have ever seen. The gorgeous sky held not one, but TWO rainbows from the downpour. Orange and blues; yellows and whites; dark grays and peaches lit up the clouds and sky as a giant orange sun made its way down to the horizon and its slumber. I kept turning and looking in my rearview mirror, finally pulling over to stop and stare at the magnificent show that Nature was putting on display for me just at the moment I was feeling defeated.

I was transformed.

Once on a very cold early August night, a college friend and I were up on a lake in Michigan with a sky full of stars and the Universe wide open. We had bundled up and taken a canoe out to a nearby deck where we were watching the meteor shower. The clear midnight sky was filled with shooting stars late into the night as we lay on the floating deck looking up. "OOO! There's one! Looklooklook! oooOOOooo! Ahhhhhh!" As it was Michigan, on a very cold early August night, my friend and I were FREEZING, including uncontrollable chattering teeth. However, we would not give up the night yet as we were tough Spartans, and no cold was going to send us home. As we lay there chattering and shaking, we began to sing a magnificent oratorio about 'being so cold but who cares because we're tough by god' and dance with our legs kicking in the air to warm up. Then, the giggles took over as we guffawed our way through the night in the middle of "OOO! T-t-there's one! Looklooklook! I'm F-F-FREEZ-ING! brrrrrrr! heeheehee! But who c-c-cares! HAHAHAHAHAAAA!!! oooOOOooo! Ahhhhhh!" I was in the middle of a lake in Michigan with a dear friend, laughing and freezing through shooting stars.

I was transformed.

I lived in Northern California while attending clown school. To earn my keep for a place to stay, I took care of two dogs named Oreo and Yin. We used to go the Pacific Ocean at Mad River Beach, a beach that was animal and people friendly. Oreo's thing was that he would drink his fill of ocean water as he splashed in and out fervently fetching a stick. Of course, he would promptly vomit it all back up as soon as he got in the car, my car, to go home. Yin, the elderly and gentler of the two, would just be happy to be included in one of our 'out and abouts.' One day, we three went out to the beach on a misty, cold day. As we came up over the dune, the mist parted to show a giant sea creature right in front of us. Oh my gosh! There was a giant bull sea lion just sitting on the beach right in front of me! As many dogs and people as there were on that beach, the amazing thing was that not one bothered this amazing creature. I can't blame them as he was IMMENSE and I didn't move (ok . . . couldn't) as I was stunned. He stayed for a while before slipping off into the ocean; vanishing as the mist covered his departure.

I was TRANSFORMED.

The moments in my life that have changed me for the better, that have transformed me, are often the gentle moments, the everyday moments. Yes, I have had huge moments in my life that have also transformed me, but usually with those moments I end up saying, 'Well, God must still want me here on this planet. Huh.' Or "What in the HELL?!?" There have been other moments that have lasted a lifetime. Moments of betrayal and abuse from the hands of 'family members' that have never made any sense and may never make any sense to me. The 'why would you do that?' will never be answered as these people have conveniently forgotten that they would ever do anything so horrid.

I have always envied those who have supportive and loving family members still in their lives to count on. While I DO have some members of my very extended family that I am close to and am able to rely on for support and laughter and love, the 'immediate' family members are not those people. These moments have taught me that family of blood is like anyone else in your life: trustworthy or weak; supportive or destructive; friendly or cruel; good or bad; kind or abusive. These moments have taught me that those I have CHOSEN as family are truth and love for me. I count myself very lucky to have many of those chosen people in my life as I look forward to including many, many more into MY family; MY choice. I have lived with immediate family members who did me harm and I have been transformed. I have chosen my TRUE family through the years, and I have been TRANSFORMED.

I have been transformed into an even better and more loving human being. Because of my chosen family, their love and humor and support, I have transformed into someone I am comfortable to be. I have transformed into someone I am to be. I have transformed into someone who I am to become.

In these gentle moments of my life, when I least expect ANYTHING yet something wonderful always happens, I have found my moments of great transformation occurring. These moments cannot be taken away from me and I hoard them and events in my soul. These gentle moments of transformation help to create who I am and who I am proud of becoming. In many ways the journey seems long and yet, through the magic and joy—the fun of it all—it has happened so fast. In the blink of an eye. In the downpour of rain or the shooting of a star. Maybe it IS as Ms. Salata speaks of in her quote. On the days that I become mired down in the exacting day-today-ness of life, I just need to shift my perspective.

I need to look from the work of life to the fun, magic and joy of life. Like I did today with the help of one small but profound cat. Today, just this morning, in an unexpected gentle moment, I watched a cardinal sipping and splashing with abandon.

I was transformed. ✾

Notes

JAN FRASER INSPIRED LIFE SERIES

Treasured

TRANSFORMATIONS

Sophia Chow

❖

Sophia Chow is the very definition of a 'self-starter'. She is a certified coach and trainer who specializes in supporting people who want to embrace a life of challenge by choice, (Re) envision thriving over surviving and reshape their mindsets to build resilience.

She has the amazing ability to help others cut through the lies of society's stories and workplace toxicity, (Re) write their own rules for living and loving life and ground into their inner wisdom and life's purpose.

Her passion is making an impact for individuals, families and communities in a world full of chaos. She believes that to dream and live our best life, we need to nourish ourselves by investing in who we want to be, what we want to feel every day, and how we want to make our impact.

Sophia is originally from China, and now lives in Charlotte, NC with her husband and son.

Contact

Email: sophiachownc@gmail.com

A 7,000 Mile Journey:
Tradition to Transformation

By Sophia Chow

*" . . . Nature makes itself even more forceful when tradition
and circumstance stand in an individual's way . . . "*

— Albert Einstein

In a strict traditional Chinese family, children follow their parents' wishes and desires. As a daughter, I needed to live close to my parents' home to take care of them as much as possible. I was also being taught by mom that to be financially independent and capable of surviving on my own was important.

After graduation from college in China, I left home, moving all the way to the U.K. to pursue my Master's degree. I didn't know anyone. This was the first time ever in my life that I made that choice to honor my own heart above the desire of my parents. This was not something people in my family did. No one in my family or extended family had ever been able to study or live outside of China.

I was the first! It was a big deal. As an international student, I studied hard to realize my dream and subsidized my tuition fee by working part-time.

In my 30's, I met and fell in love with my husband, Danny. The relationship was against my mom's wishes, because my husband wanted me to move to the United States to build our family. I remembered when my mom had a serious talk with me on a sunny Saturday afternoon after she heard the news. She was devastated. She complained about me moving out of the house and country for love. I felt scared and unloved. Once again, I made the choice to honor my love and be responsible for the transformation in my life.

After moving to the States, I worked very hard, every single day with my marriage and with my little boy to craft a new identity in a new environment. I built my personal reputation from the ground up in corporate settings. If I hadn't taken 100% responsibility for my transformation, the day-to-day happiness I feel in my marriage, with my family, and at work wouldn't be my reality.

As a mom, I will always give my beautiful son, Max, the confidence and self-assurance necessary to be who he wants to be. I will always encourage my son to purse his dreams and make them come true by stepping outside his comfort zone in ways that will make him a better person every day.

My little boy has been passionate about Marvel heroes and their ways to enhance people's lives currently. He always shouts aloud, "I'm a superhero!" It's no coincidence that the Marvel heroes who inspired me back then – Captain America. Spiderman, Iron Man – always had a little help with their suite of superpowers. These figures inspired me and caused me to wonder about their transformative abilities to imagine new futures and improve people's lives.

I've been helping people and organizations transform their lives and businesses over the last years. The greatest achievements I've witnessed have resulted from exceptional responsibility.

Transformation is about the way you think and operate as an individual or organization. It's not because of the other people, the technology itself, or something else that provides you with competitive advantage. It is you who create value, lead a more fulfilling life, and get from where you are to where you want to be.

My life experience is different from yours, which is different from the experience of others. We all have certain motivations in common:

to build, to make a difference, to make better, and in some manner, to change the world around us.

I am building a responsible life and relationships consistently because I am the CEO of me.

Even though I have doubts, I vow to be a life changer every single day, and I will do this just as bravely as when I left everything to come to the U.S. It's because of me that my family members will leave home as people of integrity, confidence, and accountability.

You may be the leader bringing people along with you into the future, or you may be a central part of that team. Your success at transforming your life, organization, and business will depend on a shared understanding of what you want to be in the world, a commitment to change, a passionate direction and effort.

There is no right way to enter into transformation. For me, I felt my most pressing need was to follow my heart.

Most often, transformation is driven by the most pressing need in your life.

Fill yourself with HOPE!! ✹

Michele Lutz

---❀---

Michele Lutz's passion is to help others find their true, authentic self by going inward and healing emotionally, which gives them the opportunity to make room for new, positive emotions. She believes that people are God's highest form of creation and if they listen to their inner guidance, practice gratitude and uncover the truth of they really are, then they can become aligned with what their soul has come here to do.

She lives in Pittsburgh, Pennsylvania and has been an entrepreneur for the last 30 years in the salon, beauty and health industry and has dedicated her life to helping her clients transform their self image so they can live their best life personally and professionally.

She has invested in her personal development by becoming a Jack Canfield Certified Success Trainer and a Reiki I & II practitioner. She has also been trained in RIM Essentials, Sound Healing and essential oils.

Contact

Website: www.michelelutzlifecoach.com
Email: michele@michelelutzlifecoach.com

Transformed Back to My True Self

By Michele Lutz

"We cannot become what we want by remaining what we are."

— Max Depree

My life wasn't always smooth sailing. My childhood consisted of my parents divorcing when I was five then it was constant upheaval after that. I lived with my mother and didn't see my father at all. Because my mother was not in a stable relationship we moved around a lot. In my first 28 years, I had moved 34 times.

Unfortunately, that made me feel like I never fit in anywhere. I spent a lot of time alone since I was an only child, and my mother was working the afternoon shift at the airlines to provide for us. She did the best she could with what she knew at the time. Looking back, I never had anyone teach me the skills to have a solid foundation in life.

The majority of my early adulthood felt like I was in survival mode – always hustling, searching for something to fulfill my inner being and always needing to be busy. I never felt like I was doing the right thing, although from the outside it looked like I had it all together. I suffered from severe anxiety and obsessive compulsive disorder but hid it well. Everything I did seemed like an overwhelming task. Surprisingly, I graduated from beauty school at 18 and began my career shortly after. I had artistic ability and loved to help people look and feel better about themselves. I purchased my first home at the age of 19 and opened my salon at age 23 when my son was only a year old. As time went on, I had another son and daughter plus three failed marriages.

I was not exactly where I wanted to be in life, but I kept pushing through.

At my lowest, I was depressed and merely existing. I was chronically involved with toxic men. I had been involved in a destructive relationship, off and on for 15 years, with a narcissist that was mentally, physically and sexually degrading and abusive. I kept trying to make it work for the sake of our daughter which ended up backfiring. He continued to brainwash her and forbade her to talk to me to this day. When being in the middle of all of that craziness, the voice inside my head kept questioning, why are you putting up with this abuse? I was beyond frustrated because I was not taking care of myself or doing any of the things that I loved to do. At that point I had been through so much trauma, I was angry and lost. I was spiraling out of control with drinking too much because I just wanted to numb myself from the pain.

Then I realized it doesn't have to be that way. So I had to ask myself is what I'm doing right now supporting the life that I want to create? I knew deep down that it wasn't and I was destined to do more. It was time to be truthful and stop lying to myself! During that time, I had a huge realization. 'You don't attract what you want, you attract what you are!'

Fortunately, I had enough self-discipline and structure to know in what direction I needed to proceed. I decided to join a 90-day "no drinking challenge," but had no idea what was about to happen next. I felt like my old self again – exercising, eating healthy food, sleeping soundly and no anxiety whatsoever. My spark and enthusiasm for life was back! After completing that challenge, I did a 10-day Life Transformation with Jack Canfield that I stumbled upon while reading his book *The Success Principles*.

That started me on my journey of becoming a Certified Canfield Success Trainer. I knew from the moment I signed up that I was on the path to living my purpose and passion because the never-ending hunger in my soul was finally being fulfilled.

I did have one big problem though. I was still angry and needed to find forgiveness . . . but how? I was open to try anything so I began with a 30-day emotional reset experience using Young Living Essential Oils. The oils have a vibrational frequency that help unlock stuck energy. When inhaled, the impulses from these oils are sent directly to the limbic system where they can mobilize long held cellular memories stored in the body. The experience included six carefully selected oils such as Valor, Harmony, Forgiveness, Inner Child, Present Time and Release. I used the oils morning and evening while saying positive affirmations then journaling about what I had experienced. I continue to use these and other oils during my meditation time or when writing in my gratitude journal.

The next thing I did was set goals for myself and created a vision board in September 2020 to help me achieve them. I focused twice daily on my board while having the feeling that I had already achieved all of these things. Some of my goals were to workout 3-5 times a week, adopt a dog, take a vacation to the beach, sign up for horseback riding lessons and spend a few weeks in Sedona. My time in Sedona was filled with self-care. The energy vortexes there are absolutely magical. I enjoyed reading, hiking, a massage and spending time with my sons.

The two most profound things that helped me with the clarity that I was searching for were my energy healing session which helped me clear any blockages in my energy chakras using Reiki and Tachyon energy. The second was my intuitive reading which opened my Akashic records. I received information about my gifts at the soul level which were channeled through my spirit guides. To experience these things gave me clarity and peace. It was the first time that my soul was filled with true, authentic love for myself. Even though I always had confidence, I lacked self-love and truly never believed I deserved more.

You might be shaking your head saying to yourself I thought they were kind of the same thing. Don't worry, I did too. Confidence is your power, strategy, fearlessness and your inspiration to others. Your self-love is your protection, GPS, boundary and best friend.

I felt that I still had more healing to do especially if I wanted to help others with their journey. Not long after thinking this, I received an email from Jack Canfield inviting some of his trainers to join him at a place called Rythmia in Costa Rica. Rythmia is a Life Advancement Center that offers meditation, yoga, breathwork, massage, plant based diet and Ayahuasca. The purpose of the ceremonies using Ayahuasca is to show you who you have become, merge you back with your soul and to heal your heart.

During my time there, I was shown that I was full of fear and anxiety. I needed to forgive myself and others that had hurt me if I wanted to heal my heart. Once I got through, I realized that I was never separated from my soul but it had just been covered up with hurt, pain and stories that I told myself. It felt like a huge weight had been lifted off my body. I knew afterwards that I needed to follow my intuition because there are no coincidences.

I love this quote on one of my oracle cards: "I release all that doesn't serve me. It's time to be the truth of who I am."

My purpose is to use my knowledge to help others heal and transform by inspiring them to get through similar things that I overcame. Healing is a journey. Most likely it won't be just one thing you do that will change your circumstance. It may be several. One thing gets you stronger for the next thing which enables you to go deeper.

Be easy on yourself! Look at all the things you have accomplished not the things you haven't. If I can do it, you can too. You need to BELIEVE and NEVER GIVE UP! ✺

Notes

Lila Larson

L ila is recognized as a vibrant speaker, Executive coach, author, corporate trainer, mentor and consultant. Lila has contributed to 1000s of people in organizations as they achieved their financial and business goals in a variety of fields including technology, business, health care and education in Canada and the USA. She has over 40+ years of experience In the corporate world where she was responsible for Leadership Development and achieving bottom-line results.

She has experience with titans in the industry, including Zig Ziglar, Tony Robbins, Wayne Dyer, Brian Tracy, James Malinchak and Jack Canfield. Applying the knowledge, strategies and initiatives in the Leadership skills gained from these powerhouse self-development leaders, she encourages and supports women to explore their dreams and recreate their future.

In her downtime, Lila loves to explore and travel North and South America, The British Isles, and the Caribbean, spending her days enjoying nature, photography and learning about people and cultures.

Contact

Website: www.lilalarsoninternational.com
Email: coachinglinks1@gmail.com

Journey to Freedom

By Lila Larson

"You and I possess within ourselves at every moment of our lives, under all circumstances, the power to transform the quality of our lives."

— Werner Erhard

It was Thursday evening, August 25, 2015, 6:30 PM just after dinner as I was leaving the TV room when he said, "Sit down, I have something to tell you." I sat facing him across the room as he lay on the couch in his usual prone position in front of the 60-inch TV.

He said, "I'm leaving you."

"Oh," I said. "When?" I asked.

"September 1, 2015," he said.

I said, "Oh. Where are you going?" I asked.

"To Selkirk," he said, "I rented a house."

"Oh," I said.

He said, "Aren't you going to ask me why?"

I said, "OK, why?"

He said, "Because I don't know what love is and I'm not happy."

I said, "Oh."

And as I said this last "oh", an overwhelming sense of relief and gratitude washed over me from the top of my head to the tips of my toes. I continued to sit and attempt to absorb what I had been told. The relief was palpable in knowing that I no longer had any responsibility to attempt to keep the 51-year marriage together. I had been struggling to find ways to "make him happy" and ways to release me from the anger, judgement, control, sarcasm, financial control, mocking my spiritual beliefs, and attempts to isolate me from friends and family.

I asked if he had told our son (who was working on the computer in my office). He said, "No."

My response was "You need to tell him as you are the one leaving." He uncurled himself from the couch, made his way to the office and was back in three minutes.

"I told him," he said resuming his prone position on the couch.

What I came to realize through a lengthy separation was that his ongoing procrastination to get a lawyer and provide the legal documentation, provided time for me to be truly free. This meant that the transformation would have to be within me!

The words of Jack Canfield popped into my mind about how I could proceed. E + R = O (Event plus response = Outcome.) Decision made: Take 100% responsibility for me and my life, starting NOW.

No longer would I hold back saying what I wanted to say in defense of myself – for what I had said or done, or not said or done.

No longer would I scramble to think of what would keep him from being angry and lashing out at me and my son.

What would keep ME safe?

I recalled the memory of what I had heard earlier that summer.

On July 31, 2015, at 1:30 PM, I had arrived home with groceries and heard my brother's voice. As I quietly approached the TV room, I peeked around the corner and saw that he was holding his cell in the air and talking to my brother on speaker. What I heard shocked me to the core.

"No, you're moving too fast. Slow down," said my brother, "No, don't take the vehicle away from her. That would not be good for you to do that. There are two parts to getting a divorce. We need to talk more about this."

I crept back down the hallway, went to the outside door, slammed it, took the groceries into the kitchen and began to put them away.

He came bounding into the kitchen saying, "I just talked to your brother."

"What's new?" I asked.

"Nothing, I need to go back to work now," he said. And he left.

I sat there stunned, filled with a certainty that the behavior I had been observing for the past several months now had an explanation. The lies, evasions, withholding of finances to pay bills all had a reason.

What did I need to do right then?

I left the house, drove to a quiet spot, called my therapist, and made an appointment. She gave me one within 10 days. My brain was a mishmash of struggling to figure out what I needed, how I felt, and the first step to take?

Tears flowed as feelings of betrayal, rejection, and anger surfaced. After supporting him through alcoholism, gambling, bankruptcy, marital cheating, cashing in three of my pension funds to bail his business out of financial situations – that NOW here I was at my age – facing no job, no savings, only government pension to live on, finding a place to stay and a way to support myself.

The way forward was going to be "THROUGH".

The lonely challenge, I was missing my three prayer warriors (my parents and my aunt) as they had died three years before.

My blessings at this time were friends, colleagues, church community, and professional associates.

I realized that I needed to find ways to shift my perspective from "Woe is me" to "How grateful I am."

The more I focused on my blessings and chose to be grateful daily for the people who listened and supported me, the more I was grateful to be alive and on my journey to freedom.

If I wanted cereal for supper at 8 PM, I could. If I wanted to offer support to a neighbor as he was working in his yard, I could do so without having to explain my actions. I enjoyed making decisions and spending time with those who cared for and about me. The freedom to decide what and when to spend money was empowering.

All of these opportunities were freeing.

It took a long time to recognize the ways that I had felt imprisoned and unsafe. I came to realize that I had been a victim of domestic abuse for years. I remembered as if it was yesterday, the time when he pulled his fist back and lunged toward me. I moved to the side and his fist smashed into the door behind me. He permanently damaged his bow and arrow fingers as a result. At the time I said, "You will only ever hit me ONCE."

The financial control, emotional abuse, mocking, judging, criticizing, verbal lashing out were all symptoms of Domestic Violence, yet, he never physically abused me.

What stopped me from breaking free and saying and doing what was right for me? I never understood.

If I had it to do again, I would have sought help from a therapist earlier, learning to speak up in a safe way, at home and at work to take action to protect myself.

I never realized how threatened he felt as I continued my graduate education and attended professional development opportunities in Canada and the USA. When I shared what I learned with him, I was rebuffed, ignored and belittled, which caused me to discontinue the efforts. I was learning so much and experiencing joy, applying those teachings in my work life and sharing with colleagues and friends. I felt safe, respected, and valued when I was away from home and ridiculed when I returned.

This was the way for me to transform my life NOW.

I took 100% responsibility for me, and as I began to assess what I needed to do, who to ask for support, ideas kept showing up.

I connected with a therapist I had not called in years. I knew I was emotional and needed help to untangle those feelings to take action and move forward.

I made an appointment with a lawyer to learn how to protect myself in the separation and divorce.

I met with a financial advisor to assess my finances. I needed to remove my name from joint accounts and transfer 50% of the balances into accounts in my name only, ensuring that I would have funds to live on in the immediate future.

After meeting with a realtor, I secured an appraisal for the current value of the house and the commercial property that was in my name.

Serving him with papers required him to provide an assessment of equipment he owned at his business. A deadline was needed for the appraisal of his property and a complete statement of his bank accounts and investments. All of this infuriated him, and he refused to comply.

As a result, it was necessary to hire a Bailiff to serve him with papers and require that he MUST provide this documentation. Included in those papers was the notice of separation and pending divorce filings. He needed to obtain legal advice in order to proceed.

The process of packing his "stuff" and notifying him to retrieve his belongings continued. I was crying at times as I watched memories leave, being donated to charities. A sense of freedom evolved as I no longer was responsible for keeping his items for him.

Researching affordable places to live with the help of a friend, we discovered a main-floor apartment facing south with entrance security and available in two months. I made a deposit and a moving date was set.

In order to sell the house, the realtor recommended numerous changes to increase the marketability. After being listed for three months with no offers, renovations began and took place over the next four months. Changing the realtor resulted in an offer within 7 days and a closing date 7 weeks later.

My journey to freedom continued over the next four years until the divorce was finalized.

What does this mean for you as you choose your journey to freedom from whatever your current situation is?
- Trust that what you are experiencing is real
- Reach out for support – therapists, friends, legal, accounting
- Set up ways to keep yourself healthy – exercise, healthy eating, address any sleeping issues
- Plan ways to treat yourself
  - Spa visits
  - Manicures, pedicures, facials
  - Hair care
  - Deep tissue massages

- Medical checkup, medication if needed
- Walking partners
- Phone connections with those who love and support you
- Journal what you are feeling as you are feeling your emotions
- Connect with those who will listen empathically as you go through your process of transformation
- Allow yourself to grieve the losses you are experiencing
- Connect with professionals who will walk with you as you journey this process

Have you ever thought or caught yourself saying:

- I can't do that....
- I've never been able to . . .
- That's never going to work . . .
- I've always done it this way . . .

What if you were to add 3 small words – whenever you catch yourself thinking or saying these limiting words . . . Add "UP UNTIL NOW!"

UP UNTIL NOW gives you permission to shift and take new actions.

UP UNTIL NOW releases old thoughts, patterns and behaviors.

UP UNTIL NOW allows fresh air to circulate and energize new choices.

When next you find yourself thinking or speaking limiting words or phrases, immediately say "UP UNTIL NOW." Start in that moment to make a difference.

Today, I am grateful to be on this side of my transformational journey. Each day is enjoyed, and I am happy for it. I continue as a lifelong learner sharing my knowledge.

Life is good! Friends and colleagues are good! God is good!

Trust that you too can create your Journey to Freedom, in whatever situation presents itself.

Fill yourself with HOPE!!

Ode to Hope
by Lila Larson

Hope is an energy of your personality. Develop it.
Hope is a choice to make every day in every situation
Hope seeks light
Hope seeks the positive
Hope seeks kindred spirits
Hope seeks solutions vs remaining in mud
Hope is a gift to be shared with others
Hope fills my soul
Hope and gratitude are partners
Hope is a muscle that strengthens with each application
Hope calls forth to the future of possibilities
Hope replaces "being stuck"
Hope is kindness
Hope unleashes joy
Hope celebrates abundance
Hope is love
Hope is our dreams
Hope speaks my truth
Hope lies in the spaces
Hope is unspoken or not
Hope is inside my heart
Hope is my world
Hope is wanting to say yes
Hope is between whispers
Hope is timeless

Regina Andler

Regina Andler is a Mindset Transformation Expert who helps women entrepreneurs move from overwhelmed to overjoyed in their business, guaranteed, using her proprietary FINDING ME™ method.

As a small business owner since 2002, Regina understands exactly what it is like to juggle running a business while juggling day-to-day life.

She is a Jack Canfield Success Principles Certified Trainer and also certified in Wholebeing Positive Psychology.

Her passion is to help women business owners create more balance and harmony in their lives by teaching them how to shift their mindset for success.

In her spare time, Regina volunteers with local non-profit organizations and she is an avid obstacle course racer.

Contact

Website: www.autumnascentconsulting.com
Email: regina@autumnascent.com

Don't Make Me Pull This Car Over!

By Regina Andler

"The most authentic thing about us is our capacity to create, to overcome, to endure, to transform, to love and to be greater than our suffering."

— Ben Okri

For some of us, one day it just happens, BOOM! You have just become the parent of your parents.

You didn't plan for this day. You didn't even think about it. Then, one event happens that changes your life forever.

Transformation happens every day of your life. It is simply about change. Most transformation comes about in small things, like finding that brand new coffee joint that is now your absolute favorite, or that new show your friend told you about that you are now obsessed with and binge watching.

Then there are those major life changing transformations that alter the trajectory of your life forever. They require you to step up and step way out of your comfort zone.

For me, a chain reaction of major transformations, both good and not-so-good, altered me in ways I would have never thought possible.

Have you ever said to yourself "If I could have a do-over, I would do it much differently."?

The lessons that I didn't realize until after the fact, may very well help you to stop, think, and do things a bit differently if you ever find yourself on a similar path.

It started in May 2000. Everything in my life was going amazingly well. My husband and I both had great corporate jobs that had benefits and income. We just finished building a brand-new home in New Hampshire that we helped design. Yes, life was good!

Moving day to our new home finished when my cell rang.

It was mom. "Dad is in the hospital. He has congestive heart failure, and they don't know if he is going to make it through the night."

Have you ever had that feeling, like they do in the movies when something bad happens and you see the person spiraling away down into the abyss? That's exactly what it felt like. My world came to a sudden standstill. I left the new home to the care of my husband and rushed to Cape Cod, MA, where mom and dad lived.

Dad was in critical condition at Cape Cod Hospital. The doctors decided that he needed to be transported to Mass General in Boston for acute care.

At this time, Mom was not in top health either and dad took care of her. With Dad in the hospital, I was now the one taking care of mom. I took time off from work and spent the next couple of weeks driving mom back and forth from the Cape to Boston.

He made it! They got him stabilized and mom and I went up to Boston to break him out of the hospital and bring him home.

Mom took the front seat and dad took the back as we started the hour or so long drive back to Cape Cod.

As soon as we hit the highway, mom started peppering dad with things to do when he got home. "Bill, there is some stuff in the garage you need to get cleaned up." "So-and-so called. You need to call them back."

Dad listened for a bit, gave a couple mumbled responses to a few questions, then finally said "For God's sake Irm! I just got out of the <insert expletive here> hospital. Give it a rest already!"

This started a tennis match of comments back and forth.

I said nothing, though my grip on the steering wheel was getting tighter and tighter.

Finally, I couldn't take it anymore. "DON'T MAKE ME HAVE TO PULL THIS CAR OVER!"

It just came out. I couldn't stop it! It was a very surreal moment in my life.

For the rest of the ride home, neither of my parents uttered a word.

All the while I was thinking "OMG . . . Did I just say that to my parents?"

It was in that exact moment, that I realized that I had just become the parent.

The next few years were a whirl wind of activity. My life completely transformed from corporate executive to caretaker. I had done well in my corporate position financially, and so I decided to quit my job and focus on the new house and taking care of my parents.

My parents seemed to make a game out of hospitalizations. Dad in 2000 for his heart, mom in for major back surgery in 2001, dad back in 2002 for something new, and so on. They literally played a game of hospital leapfrog.

By the end of 2002, things had stabilized a bit, and I decided to open my own computer repair company. It was great. I had a shop on the main drag in town, competent employees and a customer base that grew every week.

I had the flexibility to take the time to care for whichever parent happened to be on the disabled list at the time.

Once again, life was pretty good. I had a healthy balance between my business, life, and caretaking duties.

Then, in 2007, dad got sick. This time, he did not fare so well. He went into the hospital in January 2007, got out from rehab on May 5th and passed on May 20th.

At this point in time, dad was mom's primary caretaker. That role was now mine.

There were decisions to be made. Mom could not stay by herself on the Cape, and I was not moving to the Cape. Mom's conditions dictated that she would need to be in a nursing home versus assisted living and she did not want that, and I did not want that for her either.

My husband and I talked it over and mom came to New Hampshire to live with us in our home.

My caretaking duties went up to a brand-new level of care. Between my business, caring for mom full-time and taking care of the maintenance of the Cape house that she was not quite ready to part with yet, it wasn't long before I realized that something needed to change.

At this time, mentally I was not in the best frame of mind, and it was not getting any better. Without realizing it, I had stopped taking care of me as I was solely focused on mom.

By 2008 I really began to feel like I was spiraling out of control. I started a side gig with a direct sell company and as part of their training, I was introduced to the idea that thoughts were things. I watched The Secret, a movie about the Law of Attraction. I started reading books by Napoleon Hill, Wallace Wattles, Abraham-Hicks, Michael Gerber, and Jack Canfield.

None of it really sunk in, but it made me feel a little better reading it all. It made sense, it seemed, at least for other people.

In 2009, another major event happened when I made the decision to sell my business. All the juggling of the business and mom's care was taking its toll. I was now, really, a full-time caretaker.

Mom's health was deteriorating slowly, and I spent more and more time taking care of her needs. In doing so, without actually realizing it at the time, I completely stopped taking care of mine.

On May 27, 2013, mom passed away peacefully in her bed in my home. Exactly the way she wanted. It was Memorial Day. She had a great dinner of steak and homemade crab cakes, her requisite Beefeaters gin (doc okayed!) and I got her into bed, kissed her good night and she dozed off to her favorite TV show. Sometime later, she just stopped breathing.

Have you ever lost a loved one you cared for? While the event is expected to arrive at some point, you are never really ready.

For me, this event only served to drop me into a deep depression while I attended to all of the estate details that needed to be handled.

My husband was getting worried.

Day after day, he would come home from work and find me lying in mom's bed watching her favorite TV show. I just didn't want to get up and deal with the world.

It had been a total of 13 years taking care of dad and mom and over those years, I gained over 50 pounds, was not sleeping well, not eating well and certainly not exercising. Mentally I was not in a good state-of-mind.

At this point in time, the transformations that had taken place in my life were like mom and dad's hospital stays – they leapfrogged back and forth from positive to negative.

After a couple months of this, one of my close girlfriends called me and said she was going to do a race in Boston at Fenway Park. Something called a Spartan Sprint. She was insistent that I go and do this race with her (yes – she was worried about me too).

Reluctantly, I agreed. My mindset was "What is the worst that could happen? I could fall and break my neck – oh well."

I went to the registration page, signed up, and went to YouTube and searched for videos to give me an idea of what I had agreed to do. In retrospect, it was a good thing I waited until after I signed up to watch the videos!

I have never been the athletic type at any point in my life. As I watched video after video of Spartan races with wide eyes, I thought to myself 'What have you gotten yourself into!'

Turns out, watching those videos was the starting point of a transformation back to a better place.

I'm not going to lie . . . watching those videos scared the heck out of me! I was watching these athletes climb up ropes, climb over walls, swing on rings and monkey bars and a whole bunch of other things that I knew with absolute certainty I could not do.

This was the intervention I needed. I started to train with my friend. I was almost 200 pounds, and my diet was still pretty lousy, and I was definitely out of shape.

I remember going to my first training to get ready for the race, about three months before the race in November 2013 and I thought I was going to die. But I kept it up.

The Universe was on my side and pushing me to do this. Mom and dad were with me every step of the way too. I know this because both my parents were avid Red Sox fans. The race was at Fenway Park. In October 2013, the Red Sox won the World Series. It was synchronicity.

The race was also three days before my 50th birthday. A perfect time for a major life transformation.

Race day came and there were four of us in our little group. We were all new at this, so we stuck together and helped each other out. The good thing is one of the people with us was a nurse. She recognized when I stopped halfway through the race that I couldn't breathe. She helped me through an exercise-induced asthma attack. We all finished and after crossing the finish line received our finisher medals. The first thing I said, "That was awesome! I want to do it again!"

What I didn't recognize until after that first race was that in all my years as caretaker to my parents, I had completely stopped taking care of me. If I had that do-over, I would find a better balance between my parents care and my care.

And so began the next chapter in my life where I paid more attention to my diet, lost weight and continued to exercise and train for these crazy, fun, obstacle course races. My outlook on life completely transformed and at age 58 I am still racing today.

If you ever find yourself facing a similar challenge, remember that taking care of you is just as important as taking care of them.

Notes

Cherylanne Thomas

Cherylanne's passion for life has her living in the fast lane where she is most comfortable. She is a bestselling co-author and has received her MBA and several certifications focused in the area of Sales, Marketing, Executive Coaching and Leadership Development. Cherylanne serves as a senior sales and marketing executive specific to the hospitality industry and has worked for many luxury hotel brands including Ritz Carlton, Waldorf Astoria, and Hyatt Hotels and Resorts. For the past 25 years, with curiosity and passion to elevate sales and leadership teams to a higher level of performance, Cherylanne has transformed organizations toward greater success by discovering what works to increase their topline revenue. Cherylanne is a distinguished Toastmaster who has authored several white papers on luxury marketing, success principles and service excellence. She is a bibliophile, an avid sports enthusiast and volunteers in her spare time to local pet shelters. Originally from Boston, Massachusetts, Cherylanne currently resides in the Metro D.C. area.

Contact

Website: www.cherylannethomas.com

The Art of Transformation

By Cherylanne Thomas

"You and I possess within ourselves at every moment
of our lives, under all circumstances, the power
to transform the quality of our lives."

— Werner Erhard

If there was ever a moment of transformation, it is the moment we are born. In that instant we step into a new reality, that of human life and consciousness. Even at that moment we become a person with a character as unique as our DNA. Our first breath marks the beginning of our journey we call life.

Throughout our lifetime, we encounter a broad range of opportunities, challenges, and lessons from which we hope to learn. The events we experience reveal the strengths, specific talents, and characteristics we are given by our higher spiritual guide to help us evolve and become the best we can be.

I don't remember my first step, or the time I said my first word, which would account for transformations in their own right. What I do remember as a very little girl, around the age of six years old, is that I would lie in bed at night and regularly stare at the ceiling before falling asleep. It was on that ceiling that I would imagine the future I wanted to create for myself. I would look through my mother's books and magazines with their pictures, envisioning the way I wanted to dress, the places I wanted to go, and what I wanted for a career as an adult. Lying in bed and staring at the ceiling would bring all those pictures on paper to life for me. As a child, I knew it was a life I wanted to create for myself. Looking back, and before I realized who I was becoming as an adult, I knew that I was motivated and driven to constantly envision my life moving onward and upward in a constant state of positive transformation.

It is hard to look back and talk about myself as being courageous and brave but if I was listening to someone else tell my story that is exactly what I would say. So often we think of bravery as some grand gesture or a victory won. For me it began with a simple act of needing to feed my family.

I came from very humble beginnings and the worst I can remember is one day not having any food in our home. That was the day I transformed my state of mind and took it upon myself to knock upon a neighbor's front door to ask for food for my mom, my two sisters, and myself. I remember distinctly thinking that there had to be a better way than the way we were living. This means no disrespect to my mother who raised three girls mostly on her own. My mother is a proud woman who, for many years worked two jobs with no family support, and was too proud to ask for government assistance. I love, respect, and admire my mother for how she raised her three daughters.

What my action taught me is that being brave is rewarding and that people are kind. Our neighbor filled our kitchen cabinets to the brim with food for us; I was humbled and grateful.

I know that change can be hard. It requires no extra effort to settle for status quo. Auto pilot keeps us in a fixed position, but transforming our life requires continuous commitment and effort. That is where the good stuff takes place, when we push through the barriers of our comfort zone.

Pushing through those barriers came for me at the age of 17. I was the only one of the entire family who aspired to go to college. Being petrified that I wasn't smart or rich enough, I took the college boards and applied to several colleges. I received some acceptance letters but more rejection letters than I care to remember. I could have played it safe and decided to go to a school in a sleepy town outside of Boston Proper, but instead, selected a school that was located in the heart of downtown Boston. What kept coming to mind during that time were all those childhood images on the ceiling that I recalled as a little girl.

I worked through that summer, packed my bags to move to Boston in August, and never returned to live in New Bedford, Massachusetts. I closed that chapter and went in search of a better life. Looking back, this was an act of major transformation; I matured quickly. I learned that I had to fully support myself and began to save money to pay off my college loans that would become due after I graduated. One of my vivid childhood memories was my dream to work in a big city, and I manifested that for myself. That first semester I took on a full academic course load along with two part time jobs as a bartender and a filing clerk. Not realizing it fully, I recall feeling like a caterpillar transforming into a butterfly and it exhilarated me!

As I mentioned earlier, transformation can come through many opportunities and challenges. As we grow older we inevitably experience both. It was at the age of 19 that I met the love of my life. His name was Jor and we had nine plus wonderful years together before he died. I had never experienced death in such a traumatic way. Jor was sick for exactly six months and four days before I lost him. He initially suffered a severe stroke that led to the discovery of a deadly brain tumor. I know that he lived a short time after the stroke merely to give me and his loved ones time to prepare for the inevitable.

I remember so clearly when we said our goodbyes. It was a sunny brisk day on November third around three o'clock in the afternoon. I had brought Jor out on the porch in his wheelchair to get some fresh air while I unpacked the car of groceries. I vividly recall that as I was coming up the walkway, toward the house, our eyes locked. Not a word was spoken between us but, in that instance, our eyes communicated everything. Jor's eyes told me that he was exhausted and my eyes replied I was ready to let him go. The following day at 9:14 am Jor died at home. As much as he gave me the time to prepare for his death, I still wasn't ready. It took over three years to mourn the loss of my husband. This was the first time that I experienced a transformation through heartfelt, aching pain.

After six years, I was blessed to find another good man and a different kind of love. Norman and I were married for 14 years before we divorced. Upon reflection, I realized our divorce could have been preventable, but this is the kind of wisdom that comes from hindsight and maturity. Nonetheless, it led to another transformative painful experience.

Failure is often associated with divorce and I went into a deep depression before seeking professional help. Unfortunately, mental depression is prevalent in my family. Discovering that my biological father committed suicide by shooting himself in the head, followed by losing my youngest sister and my niece to drug overdoses, I knew I needed to gain insight into my own dark and painful emotions.

The next few years after my divorce were a blur. I was falling into a dark place and I didn't like it. I knew I had to muster the strength to crawl my way back to the light. Admitting that I was clinically mentally depressed was both shameful and embarrassing to myself, much less sharing this publicly and with family and friends. I did not want to be judged and carry with me the stigma of mental depression. Looking back, I am proud of myself for seeking professional care. I celebrate that I have become an advocate to help people who are clinically diagnosed with mental depression, and I realize it takes more courage to seek care and share, than to remain silent and hidden.

Ten years later, I am proud to say that I am blessed with a great life. I have created a successful career in the hospitality industry; specifically, sales and marketing for luxury and upscale hotel brands all over the country. My profession has been very rewarding, despite the pandemic that paralyzed our country for nearly two years. I have gained tremendous satisfaction from mentoring associates to dream big and reach for the stars in their own lives.

Every challenge I have faced has transformed me, making me stronger and wiser. My transformations have brought me to where I am today; a place of total commitment to achieve and exceed my childhood dreams.

As they say in my Jewish faith, "L'chaim": to a life of joy and transformation. ✹

Notes

Sally Huss

Sally Huss is no stranger to transformation and change. She transformed herself from a tennis champion (World #1 Junior and Wimbledon Semi-finalist) to an entrepreneur with interesting stops along the way.

She worked in television, then in film for Samuel Goldwyn, Jr., and managed Paul Simon's music publishing company for a time.

These were outside changes. The big ones were inside. Discovering the spiritual side of life, wise and enlightened people came into her life.

One of these was a man from Hallmark Cards. He discovered Sally's tennis talents and more importantly her heart-felt artistic talents. They married in Aspen and had a son. This happy duo led to the creation of 26 Sally Huss Galleries across the county and eventually to an extensive line of children's books, all written and illustrated by Sally. She and her devoted husband of 46 years continue to: Dream big, Plan well, Work hard, Smile always . . . knowing that good things will happen!

Contact

Website: www.sallyhuss.com

Dare to Change

By Sally Huss

*"What we once enjoyed and deeply loved we can never lose,
for all that we love deeply becomes a part of us."*

— Helen Keller

Transformation. Change. Adaptation. Growth. It seems my life has been nothing but this, perhaps yours, too.

I live in the lovely state of Colorado in a charming neighborhood in Colorado Springs called Pleasant Valley. It's right next to the magnificent Garden of the Gods Park with its stunning red rock outcrops. There must have been a big change that occurred when these magnificent monoliths sprung from the earth, millions of years ago.

The only thing that has not changed in my life through the years is my marriage. Yes, the marriage has changed outwardly from a whirlwind romance in Aspen, Malibu and La Jolla to a more settled life where we presently reside. But, the man in the marriage has not changed, except for a few wrinkles. He is the same wonderful, steady, devoted husband that I married forty-six years ago. In all that time we have moved twenty-three times. Neither of us batted an eye at the changes that were necessary.

So you see, I am a pro at transformation. I am also a Gemini, which makes it easy to be flexible and adaptable when life calls for change.

When my husband and I started out together in the 70's, we built a magnificent tennis club in Aspen for a man out of New York. Two years later with a new baby in tow, I wanted out of Aspen with its racy culture. We decided on California and also decided to build our own resort/club in the hills near San Diego. Land was purchased. Architectural plans were drawn up. Various building permits were gathered. Money was spent. After one year of effort and maneuvering, the loan documents to create this complex were finally ready to be signed. All we had to do was drive to Palm Springs and sign them.

The night before this trip, I had a dream. It said, "Use your talents." I immediately knew it did not mean tennis. I had been a tennis champion at an early age (U.S. and Wimbledon Junior champion, Wimbledon semi-finalist in the Women's division). The dream meant something else.

So when Marv sat down for breakfast the next morning I said, "I'm not signing." In most marriages this would have been a deal breaker.

My loving husband calmly asked, "Then what are we going to do?"

"Art!", I said.

We sold the property and struck out in another direction. I had never thought of becoming a professional artist, although I had graduated from USC in Fine Art. However, when my loving Marv, who had been head of advertising and promotion for Hallmark Cards, assessed my art, he directed our energies into creating a line of 'Sally Huss Galleries' across the country. The final total was 26 with one gallery in Tokyo and another in Bern, Switzerland.

I was the designer and Marv was the promoter and handled the business end of things. My task was to fill these galleries with original paintings, prints, and a variety of licensed products. Those products included books of wallpaper, children's bibs (over 100), a T-shirt line, a clothing line, stationery of all kinds, purses and totes galore, pens, mugs, dishware, plus a few products that I have forgotten. On top of that, I agreed to write and illustrate a daily syndicated newspaper panel for King Features. It was called "Happy Musings." This consisted of a daily thought with a little decorative colored art to go with it.

All rolled along smoothly for several years with me up to my ears in paint and Marv up to his ears with requests from folks who wanted to put one of these happy stores in their town. Then, 9/11 hit and retail crashed. One by one these galleries closed until we were left with only one small gallery on a side street in La Jolla, which I ran.

Soon after, we had to say goodbye to our lovely garden home in La Jolla. Our condo on the golf course at PGA West also went. What were we to do next?

It was about that time that my friend, Jan Fraser, whom I had done some design work on a book she was writing, not only suggested but insisted that I go to a Jack Canfield weeklong seminar in Arizona. Through her maneuvering and generosity she made it happen.

I was sick that week, really sick, but soldiered on. I'm sure no one wanted to sit next to me. Yet it didn't seem to bother me, I was there to learn and I was going to make the best of it.

The critical stage of the event occurred near the end of the week. Jack in his wise and gracious manner led the 250 participants in a meditation, which carried each of us across a meadow to the base of a magnificent mountain. On top of the mountain a golden angel stood holding a box. In the box she held each person's life purpose. Now who wouldn't want to know that? When she opened the box for me out poured the contents, a waterfall of books. Books upon books. So that's what I was to do! I was to write books. That's what was next on my/our life path.

But, what kind of books? A dream came to me and filled out that prophecy. In the dream I was a passenger in a car that was crossing a bridge. On the sidewalk of the bridge children lay one after the other. I looked out the window and said to the driver, "Children are in danger. Why isn't someone helping them?" The car stopped. I got out and picked one child up in my arms. I said, "Children are so easy to uplift."

So that was it. I was to write children's books!

We turned a corner in our lives again. With no homes and no galleries, we were in a sense "homeless." That's when an old friend of mine Bob Abbott, a hugely talented artist, who painted under the name of Jerome Gastaldi, invited us to live on his art ranch in the hills near Fallbrook, California.

Bob and I had always seen eye to eye on spiritual matters and art, and I had even given his wife the formula for finding her life partner. She got Bob! (I have finally written a book revealing my formula *How to Find Your Soulmate.*) The time spent on this property was magical. The air was clean, the oaks and avocado trees filled the hillside, except where Bob had created areas for visiting groups to lunch or paint. There were large spaces cleared for Bob to work on his 100 foot-long paintings that would eventually be hung in Yard House Restaurants around the country. Interesting people came and went, but the most interesting of all was Bob himself. He was the most creative and generous person that I have ever met.

He offered us a rustic, little cottage to live in and a room in the main house for my computer where I could write.

E-books became the rage at that time. While Marv read every book available on self-publishing, I taught myself how to draw on the computer. Nothing fancy, yet perfectly appropriate for illustrating the stories I was writing. I had always wanted to write children's books, but the demands of the galleries never gave me the time I needed. Now I had it.

When the first book was finished (*The Little Leprechaun Who Loves Yellow*), I figured out how to self-publish it on Amazon's KDP. I stayed to the same formula of size and shape for each, adding a new book almost weekly. Again, this was early on in the e-book/print-on-demand era, and my books were well received and profitable. One book led to another. I would start a story not knowing where it would lead and when I reached the end I would be as surprised and delighted as any child who might read it. It just tickled my heart to create these books.

The number of books in my catalog has grown to well over 100, including multicultural books; books for military children; books to alleviate childhood fears; books to develop self-confidence and a positive attitude in kids. There is even a book for young children about the dangers of smoking, drinking and drug use. There is a book to explain food allergies to kids, and one or two about the importance of kindness. There are also books for every holiday. Monkeys, cows, mermaids, princesses, alligators, llamas and koalas dance across these pages telling their tales. I've worked with Head Start programs in San Diego and Denver. I'm sure there are more opportunities for the use of these books. Hopefully, I will find them.

With the deluge of self-published books hitting the market monthly (over 60,000), the pool is diluted. This is where marketing comes into play. I'm sure a marketing genius will show up one day and know exactly how to get these books into the hands of a multitude of children who will read them and love them. Until then, I'm playing pickleball!

As our adventures have taken us to Colorado, where many family members reside, I have done what I've always done with a change of location, I find my friends whom I have yet to meet. In this case, it started with a small neighborhood park where we live. I watched a group of middle-aged women having the time of their lives on a marked up tennis court playing something I'd never seen – pickleball. They were laughing and swinging paddles at whiffle balls in the oddest ways. I elbowed my way into the game and that was it: friends for life.

Six months later I completed a simple book on this fantastic sport. It's called *Dare to Dink: Pickleball for Seniors or Anyone Else Who Wants to Have Fun*. Today I teach this game to members and visitors at the spectacular Garden of the Gods Resort and Club. My dance card is filled with playdates and lessons with friends and friends to be who have dared to dink or will. Because of it, I look forward to every day.

How did I come by this attitude of welcoming change and transformation?

I believe it started with my father who planted the seed of a champion in me. In this case, it was tennis. But there were qualities of a champion that went along with this drive: the love of learning, striving, focusing, making an effort, and accomplishing are just a few. Besides this, I have always had the sense that life itself has our back if we just dare to reach out, try something new and trust it.

I have welcomed every move we've made in location and business with anticipation and excitement. I know there are nuggets in every new adventure: new opportunities, new growth, and especially new friends.

If there is one piece of advice I could give someone it would be: Dare to Change!

JAN FRASER INSPIRED LIFE SERIES

Triumphant
TRANSFORMATIONS

Sarah McCalden

Sarah McCalden is a money and business coach, and Success Principles mentor and trainer. She helps people release their fears around money, earn the money they deserve and create their most fully expressed lives. She also works with colleges and schools to provide for their staff and students through self-esteem and success education programmes that produce results.

Sarah overcame a life-threatening addiction in her 20's and got a second chance at life. This second chance has influenced her greatly in the years since and has allowed her to create a truly exciting and wonderful life.

Sarah lives in Newcastle, UK with her Kiwi husband, two sons and their cat, enjoying the best of city life, the beach and the countryside.

Contact

Website: www.sarahmccalden.com
Emai: sarahmccalden@gmail.com

From Heroin to Heroine

By Sarah McCalden

"Persistence will get you everything you want.
Keep going. You can do it. Yes you can."

— Sarah McCalden

I had three years clean and sober before the first time I tried heroin. I had graduated the university a couple of months before and had moved back home to London from Washington, DC. I thought it would be one time only. I didn't realise what I'd set in motion, until it was too late. I didn't realise the depths of despair, helplessness, hopelessness, and mental torture that addiction would take me to, but by a miracle, I survived it.

After three and a half years of stealing, cheating, lying, relapsing and having nothing on my mind at all, other than getting and us-ing more drugs, I decided I couldn't go on. I had resigned myself to using until I died. I had proven to myself that I could not get clean and sober. I had tried a hundred times over the years, and just couldn't do it, and sometimes, I didn't even want to do it. I wanted to get clean when I was high. And when I wasn't high, I needed to get high so I wouldn't get sick. I was anxious every moment, and most days, I didn't want to wake up for fear of those darkest of thoughts that just wouldn't leave me. I felt like my body did things that my mind was telling me I didn't want to do. I was in a desperate situation, and I wanted to die. I wanted it to stop.

My failed attempt at suicide March 6, 2006, and subsequent detox from heroin was not the end of my drug use, but it was the beginning of the end.

I was ashamed, distraught and felt infinitely unworthy. I couldn't even bring myself to go back to Cocaine Anonymous, but I did decide I needed somewhere to go. I started going to AA and met Katherine. We became great friends and saw each other every day. We were both newly clean and sober and we stuck together. I managed to get a lengthy period of sobriety under my belt thanks to her friendship that year, and I will always be grateful. But after nine months, self-sabotage crept back into my life and I ended up back at his house, handing him cash, saying, "Go, get some drugs."

The difference this time, was that I did ask for help and although I did relapse that night, I didn't allow myself to keep relapsing.

A few months later, I went to New Zealand with a friend who I had met in Cocaine Anonymous. I started drinking and smoking marijuana, and after a few months, I met a guy from my travels. He offered me crystal meth, and in that moment, in my mind, I came to a crossroads. Did I want to go down the path of total self-destruction again or did I want to show myself how great I could be? I burst into tears, said "No," and told him he had to take me home. He did.

And that was the last day I ever thought that doing drugs was for me.

I didn't suddenly have my life all worked out and perfect. It took many years, mistakes, lots of self-inquiry, figuring out who I really was and what I really wanted. I did a lot of growing up in New Zealand, between the ages of 28 to 35, and there were lots of challenging times ahead, but I never picked up a drink or a drug.

I chose to work on myself instead.

I started making better decisions and over time, I became more responsible and started to enjoy my life more. When my first son was born, I found within me, a deep desire to take care of this little baby and show him lots of love. I wanted to provide the best life I could for our family. Two years later, his brother was born completing our family.

My husband, however, was an alcoholic. I hated this so much about him that he chose alcohol over us. I sometimes forgot that he had an illness, the same as me. It felt like he was being mean, spiteful, irresponsible, and didn't love us. But I didn't leave him. Without realising it, I was enabling him.

In 2012, I started running for my health and fitness. It helped me deal with life and gave me focus. If I went out first thing in the morning, I would never miss a day. He was reliably at home in the mornings, and yet I could not count on him being home in the evenings. I refused to let him control my running, and over time, I achieved marathoner and ultra-marathoner status.

I proved to myself I could do anything.

The only time I went away and left my children was for a short weekend trip in February 2014. Since I was always caring for our children, I decided to visit Melbourne for the weekend by myself. The boys were two and four years old. When I got back, I found big black bags full of beer cans in the trash. He'd had a party, while I was away. Later I found out my friends had to babysit him and our children because he got high during breakfast, and they couldn't leave him alone with the children with a good conscience. When my friends told me this, I knew I needed to return to England to start the divorce proceedings. I also knew that I could be prevented from leaving New Zealand with my children even for a holiday if I left him there. He could make it difficult legally for me. I made a plan and by August that year, we had all moved to London.

As my relationship with my husband continued to deteriorate, and he continued to drink, I decided to expand the things I did to please myself. I decided that I wanted to go back to the university in 2015 to get a master's degree. We moved from a rented house to a rented apartment to pay my tuition. The Master's required intense focus, and I found myself working all day and into the evenings. Sometimes arriving home at 9pm and my children were already asleep.

By 2017, things were coming to a head. I finally wanted out of my relationship. I had been complaining about this relationship for years, and nothing had really changed. It was embarrassing, complaining about it repeatedly and not doing anything about it. I was enabling his behaviour.

I realised it was the fear of poverty that was keeping me stuck. How could I afford to leave him? I felt like I would be resigning myself to a life of poverty with my boys. I also didn't like the school system. I had been working in schools and didn't like what I saw, and desperately wanted to home educate my sons. I hated that I didn't see them as much as I wanted to. We were all missing out. I realised that even with a master's degree, I wouldn't be able to earn what I needed to live my best life as a single parent. I wanted to create a much better life for us, and I knew it had to start with me earning much more money. More money equalled more freedom of choice.

I started asking myself questions, "Why can't I be rich? What's the difference between me and someone who is wealthy?" As I was asking myself these questions, I came across a business opportunity. An opportunity I thought could help me to create the wealth I needed. I made the decision to join this company in December 2017 and sure enough, my 5th month in the business, I earned $10,500 USD – about £7500. That was more money than I'd ever dreamed of making in a month. I continued over the next two years to make this amount consistently. That first year, I made 10 times my previous income.

What changed for me? How did I go from heroin addiction to ultra-marathon runner, from earning £15,000 a year part time, to 10 times that in a year?

In early 2018, I joined the Bob Proctor Coaching programme and I started to learn about how my mind worked. I was studying this material as I was building my business. I learned that my thoughts are things. That having negative thoughts would attract negativity into my life. This one simple concept helped me to understand what I had been attracting my whole life. And having positively focused thoughts, would attract positivity into my life. I took my thoughts off my husband and put them squarely onto my business and my sons. I didn't think how I can't. I thought about I can. And I did what it took. I had blinders on, and I only saw people winning. I learned about my self-image and how the way I thought of myself really was key to creating the reality I truly desired. I shed all that self-loathing. That low self-worth, low self-esteem, poor self-concept started to melt away. In its place stood compassion, self-love, self-confidence, self-belief:

a knowing, that I could do it – whatever it was, that I wanted to do.

I looked back on my life and I recognised my persistence. I beat my heroin addiction, I achieved my marathoner and ultra-marathoner title, and I moved my family across the world. I recognised my strength and that my results were changing, which propelled me further towards my goals. I realised that I needed to celebrate all my successes, no matter how big or small.

As expected, an abundance of money gave me freedom to choose things I wouldn't be able to choose otherwise. As I started to earn more and more money, I started to feel confident in my ability to keep earning that level of income. I had the peace of mind I needed to finally confront my husband and tell him I wanted officially out of our marriage. I started divorce proceedings in June 2019. Things got worse. He started drinking even more and tried to collect the children one day in that state. I had to say no. I had time to think about what I really wanted for myself, for my children and for him. I remembered how I behaved in active addiction, and I knew if he could get clean and sober, he could turn his life around, just like I had. I remembered how I felt zero hope for me, and against all odds, I survived and created a great life for myself. I knew he could have that too.

I called him and told him I would give us another chance. I told him I wanted a dad that the boys could be proud of. I told him to quit his toxic job, quit drinking, and quit smoking drugs and cigarettes. I told him to come with us on our holiday to the States. I wanted him to figure out what he wanted and what his passions were, and if he did those things, we could talk about him moving back in, after we returned.

Choosing to give us another chance, on my terms, was the best decision I could have made.

My husband has been clean and sober ever since. We have become the team I always dreamed we could be. It's not always easy, but we work on our relationship daily. We are supportive of each other and want the very best for each other. He found his passion as an artist and I am living my passion, helping others on their path to wealth and to achieve more success in their lives.

I inspire people around the globe to earn more money and create success in their lives. I support young people in home education and in schools and colleges in the UK, with a view to expanding this service abroad. Our children are home educated and have a positive social life. We are part of a community of compassionate, confident and success-oriented people.

I love having the tools to work through my challenges in a positively focused way. My perspective matters. I will attract into my life, the focus of my attention. Remembering always where I started, my journey, and the transformation that brought me here.

I really couldn't ask for a better life. ✿

Notes

Victoria Chadderton

Victoria Chadderton is an author, trainer, speaker and Distinguished Toastmaster. She works with transformational leaders training, facilitating workshops and retreats. She is an Amazon Best Selling author. Her work with the Law of Attraction has brought out her passion for helping others visualize and obtain what brings them JOY!

In addition, she has been active in local community organizations, such as Boy Scouts of America, Washington Elementary PTSA and Women's Service League. Currently she is the District Director of District 9 Toastmasters. Victoria lives in Washington State and enjoys spending time with her family, going on family vacations and exploring new places.

Contact

Website: www.victoriachadderton.com
Email: chadderton.victoria@gmail.com

Finding My Voice

By Victoria Chadderton

"It took me quite a long time to develop a voice,
and now that I have it, I am not going to be silent."

— Madeleine K. Albright

All four of them were staring at me, waiting for me to answer their question, "Why should we choose to work with this company?"

My palms were sweating as the room started closing in on me. Thoughts were darting in and out of my consciousness. My palms started sweating the room closing in on me. Was I experiencing my first panic attack? What do I do? How do I get out of this situation FAST? I managed to get some sort of answer out with a lot of "um's" and "Ah's" and I am sure that it was not a convincing statement as to why our company was the best option for them.

I had been working for this company for a few months. When I started, I thought that it was going to be a perfect match. I would be working with people as a job coach. These individuals had been identified as having barriers to successful employment and I was the person to help them learn their job duties and build communication between them and their employer. I did not realize my job duties included company marketing and sales.

I had always been the type that would be in a conversation, and someone would ask me a question, I would say something to answer and then we would go on about our day. Of course, after they walked away and went on to the next conversation, I would come up with all the ways that I could have answered. Suddenly, the words and thoughts would be so clear to me. However, this was always after the conversation opportunity had passed.

After that ill-fated sales meeting, I went back to the office and broke down.

All the usual negative self-talk started, "Why didn't you speak up? They are never going to hire you. You can't even put a sentence together." On and on it went. I had to have this job because I had just separated from my husband, and I needed the income to support my three boys and myself. I took this job because I wanted one that allowed me to be of service to others and help them achieve the life that they wanted. I am a great cheerleader and want the best for people. My pity party lasted the rest of that day.

When I went home, I knew that I needed to figure something out. If not, I was going to be in a miserable job, unable to provide decent service or possibly even get fired.

I had heard of Toastmasters throughout my life and had met a couple people who were members. Even though I was terrified to go to a local club meeting I decided to go and see if this was the solution to my problem. I knew exactly where the local club met because it was in the same church basement that my scout troops met. From another room, I used to watch people getting up and speaking in front of the group. I could never hear what was being said but I watched. No one ever fainted (or worse) had their guts explode due to fear. Everyone left with a smile on their face, and they seemed friendly enough as I passed them on the stairs going to our respective meetings.

I walked into the new, but familiar, room for the first time. I was greeted by some members and they seemed nice enough. They asked my name and why I was visiting. I gave them the generic answer, "I just wanted to see what Toastmasters is all about." They handed me an agenda for the meeting and said I could sit wherever I wanted. The meeting started and they proceeded to follow the agenda. So far so good.

They came to the portion of the meeting that is called Table Topics. That is where members get to practice extemporaneous speaking. The Table Topics Master explained how this portion of the meeting would progress. The Table Topics Masters asks a question and the calls upon a person to answer. The person has one to two minutes to answer the question, and then the mic is handed to the next person. The Table Topics Master said that he would first ask a few other people to speak so that I could see how the process went. Then he would ask me if I wanted to give it a try. I watched and the questions were straight forward and those called upon to answer did so without fainting.

When asked if I would like to try, I decided to go for it. That is the reason I was there. I might as well see if I can do it. I do not remember what the question was, I do not remember what I said. I do know that I only spoke for 27 seconds and probably had 30 "um's and ah's" in my answer. I sat back down. "Well, I survived", I kept telling myself. At the end of the meeting members congratulated me on my attempt and said that they hoped to see me again. I was given a guest packet with information about Toastmasters and an application to join.

Little did I know that this night was the beginning of my transformation.

The next week I was back for another meeting with membership application in hand. Every week I took on different meeting roles and participated in Table Topics. Over time it became easier to answer the questions. My time eventually increased to the allotted amount of time, and I had less and less "um's and ah's". I did not jump into giving prepared speeches for a few months. But when I did present a prepared speech, it went OK! As it turned out, I was overthinking the entire process. However, I enjoyed the weekly meetings. Everyone was supportive and wanted the best for each other.

As I grew in my speaking abilities, I joined additional groups and started to take on leadership roles. I am currently serving as a District Director within Toastmasters. These leadership roles have helped me continue to progress in my development.

I've always wanted to be a professional speaker talking about living a life that you want. With the help of the Toastmasters program, I am developing those skills on a regular basis.

I decided that the job coach position was not for me and returned to my previous career in Tax Preparation. This allowed me the time and flexibility to pursue my dream of professional speaker.

Through various self-development courses I found that one thing I love to do is train trainers. Helping them craft their message and get it out into the world brings me joy. Watching potential trainers progress also reminds me of how far I've come from the days when I was afraid to speak up. I love being able to give back to the training community.

Another way I have 'found my voice' is by becoming a best-selling author. I have participated in numerous collaborative books that have become Amazon best sellers. In the process of writing, I've realized that I do have stories to tell and a message that can help other people in their life's journey.

Back in 2008 if you were to tell me that I was going to transform into a speaker, trainer and author, I would have thought that was far from my reach. However, through persistence and tenacity, I have transformed into a confident speaker and use my skills to help others live the life of their dreams.

Now when someone asks, "Why should I hire you?" I can answer them with confidence, knowing I can deliver. ✿

Notes

Artemis-Pallas Liontas

────── ⚙ ──────

Artemis-Pallas (everyone calls her Artemis) is the founder of a boutique consulting business in Athens, Greece where she lives. Her goal is to consult, coach and train Small Business Owners and Corporate Executives become successful in their work, business and life.

With a Bachelor in Marketing Management and an MBA from the University of Indianapolis, she worked for years in the corporate world reaching the positions of Director in Marketing, Sales and Business Development in Greek and International corporations before she decided to start her own business. Having realized that people fail in business or career because they sabotage themselves, she became a certified executive coach and a Jack Canfield Success Principles trainer to guide her customers to success.

Her talents are presenting to an audience, organizing events and turning a perplexing situation into success. In her free time you can find her doing yoga, swimming and travelling around the world.

Contact

Website: www.artemislionta.gr
Email: aliontas@karart.net

Finding Me

By Artemis-Pallas Liontas

*"Change is inevitable, but transformation
is by conscious choice."*

— Heather Ash Amara

I never expected my working life to undergo so many transformations.

When I graduated from the University, I had a dream: to conquer the world of business. And when I started working, I thought that if I worked hard enough regardless of the hours I devoted, I would be able to reach the highest levels of the corporation that hired me. In Greece we say "When people make plans, God laughs." Well, it was true. The Universe, the male business environment and my independent mentality, had other plans for me.

Working Hard was Not the Way to Get Promoted

"Artemis, come here. I want to talk to you," said my manager. He called me into his office and with a serious face said, "We agreed that you will be the one responsible for the creation of the magazine. But listen carefully. If you don't succeed, there won't be a position for you here."

I was 25 years old and the task was the creation of a magazine that was going to act as an anti-attrition tool for our customers. I had been employed by a big international corporation and I was looking forward to climbing the ladder of success. I expected to stay there my entire working life.

After two years that I had worked long hours doing mostly irrelevant things (because the position I was hired for shortly ceased to exist), the moment I was given my first opportunity to prove myself, someone had decided to cut my wings instead of encouraging me. I was devastated. My heart sunk. How can I create a magazine? I had no idea! I went to my house and with tears in my eyes I told my father about the incident. "What am I going to do? What if I don't have a job in two months? Or what if they send me to the warehouse with the rats?" (There was no warehouse and no rats, of course, but I wanted to make a point!).

"Honey, what are you talking about? There is no such option. Go and prove your worth," my dad said. Thank God he was there. It was a huge task. I did it and even though I expected to get a congratulations ceremony, a promotion and an increase in salary, none of these happened. I got something different, and more valuable as it turned out. I had started building my self-confidence. I remembered what Eleanor Roosevelt had said "No one can make you feel inferior without your permission." I was determined not to allow anyone to make me feel that I was not able to do something. Two days later, I was asked to prove my worth again.

This was the first of many incidents that occurred throughout my 15-year career as an employee and even though I managed to reach a position as Director, the process was definitely not filled with roses. In a working environment comprised almost entirely of men with grey suits and serious faces that hardly ever smiled, to simply be good at what you do is not enough to get noticed and promoted. I had to "imitate" male characteristics in order to be accepted and to find ways to look older, like to wear my glasses all the time even though it was not necessary. Opinions were not acceptable, especially when they disagreed with the "big ones." Feelings and vulnerability could not be exhibited either, and I was too independent. I had an opinion and I wanted to take the initiative, something unacceptable.

The only thing that never went away was my fear of getting fired. There were three things that I did not know, and I found out the hard way in the process.

The first was a phrase a keynote speaker had said some years later at an event I attended. "In the following years you won't necessarily evolve in the same organization and you won't practice the thing you have studied but you may need to change several positions or change your job completely." I could not have felt more relieved when looking for a job. Head Hunters tried to convince me that it would have been a mistake to build a career by changing companies and that it would have been wiser to stay in the same organization and aim for a promotion.

The second was regardless how much you work, if you don't communicate your efforts and results, you won't receive credit for it. What I did was isolate myself trying to do my job as best as possible hoping that top management would notice me and acknowledge my work. Also, as most women do, I had the tendency to present the things I was doing and my achievements as "small." I never mentioned how I managed to achieve the desired results or even how I dealt with failures. I was afraid. I minimized my work, I minimized myself. Even if the work I did significantly helped the efficiency of the business, I could not take the credit. How could top management know how different and worthy of promotion I was? I later saw that the male population around me didn't miss an opportunity to develop a network and promote even their smallest achievements. As I know now, it is a leader's characteristic to feel comfortable coming forward and being visible.

The third thing I did not know then was that I had to build my brand. Jeff Bezos, the founder of Amazon said "Brand is what people say about you when you are not in the room." I had a degree in marketing management. I knew how to promote products and services but it never crossed my mind to promote myself, to see myself as a "brand."

I decided to give myself promotions by looking for better positions in another company and then another. Similar experiences occurred. Too many hours of work, no personal life, someone else would always get the seat I wanted. I wished I had somebody (a mentor or a coach) to talk about boundaries, work life balance and the value of staying healthy.

I began to understand that I was not in the right path.

The Last Straw

As I was growing older, I was convinced that it would be harder to find another position because I was planning to be married and get pregnant. That was something unacceptable if I wanted to maintain a career. Most companies in Greece were unwilling to hire or promote women with small children.

And the worst was that my work had taken over my entire life. Even customers were asking me why I worked so much and they were wondering if I were a partner instead of just an employee. "Since you are working so hard why don't you create your own company instead of working for somebody else?" they asked me.

I was constantly tired, my face looked much older, I had practically lost all my friends since I hardly ever saw them and the worst, I was pushing myself too hard. My health had started showing worrying signs. I had palpitations which lasted a couple of hours during which I was not able to function properly, I slept fewer hours, my stress had reached higher levels and I experienced constant headaches. I was experiencing a serious burn out.

How did I create that? How did I allow it to happen? As Jack Canfield taught me in one of his trainings: What was I doing to cause such a behavior which was the same regardless if I changed environments? What parts of my life did I want to fill by working this way? Maybe I was not suitable for an employee relationship. I realized that the future I had imagined did not exist. I would hardly move beyond the middle management level, even if I did not leave the office at all, even if I did not get married.

My Own Business – A Hard Tale but I Felt Great

I decided to take the biggest risk of my life and become self-employed. I was risk averse and this was one characteristic that has held me back. It was a female characteristic that most women didn't realize. I adored my comfort zone and I was not particularly willing to leave it even though at times it didn't seem like comfort at all. What I did was complain about it.

Somewhere in between all this, I met my future husband. It was difficult to arrange a date with him. One time he said, "With all the hours that you are working, you must be earning a lot of money."

"Not necessarily," I said, slightly embarrassed.

"Then why do you do it?" he asked. "You must learn to work smarter, not harder."

Easier said than done! I had no idea what working smart was. But everything was going smoothly. I had managed to set up an office and hire a couple of free lancers to use when I needed creative support. Customers had started coming in and asking me to help them develop and promote their business.

And suddenly everything collapsed. Economic crisis hit Greece and within a fortnight all of my customers decided to cut the marketing consulting expense leaving me with no revenue and a dark future. I was devastated again. The fear of being "without a job" meaning without income appeared once again now more intense than ever.

It was around that time I discovered a book called The Success Principles by Jack Canfield. I was looking for answers again. I had to stop blaming the economy and start looking for options to rejuvenate my business and start producing again. I joined business and women organizations, I started using social media and proposing them as a marketing tool to attract customers and kept reading the book. I realized that companies needed my consulting services because they did not know how to continue to grow their business even though they were still unwilling to pay for it. Helping them, even without getting paid, filled me with enthusiasm and joy.

A New Me

"When you change the way you look at things, the things you look at, change" Wayne Dyer said. It was definite. The only thing I needed to change was myself, my mindset, my limiting beliefs. While I haven't abandoned my consulting business, I decided to become a certified executive coach and later a certified Jack Canfield Success Principles trainer.

I haven't conquered the world of business and I probably never will. I have conquered myself, my self-esteem, my creativity, and my new passion to help people transform their businesses, their careers and their lives.

As I read somewhere "Life is too short to do work that doesn't matter to you."

Don't you agree?

Notes

Paddy Briggs

For over 20 years, Paddy Briggs has been a Practice Management Consultant & Trainer specializing in working with dentists and their teams. She combined her knowledge of business, and customer service philosophy to create and refine practical, effective strategies that assist dentists in growing their business and delivering the highest level of patient care.

In 2019 Paddy graduated as a Certified Transformational Coach and a Success Principles Trainer with the Canfield Group. Through reinventing herself, Paddy became passionate about working with women. Her focus is coaching and empowering women who are in transition in either their business, career or their personal life. She inspires women to become all they were meant to be and to "live their best life".

Paddy lives on beautiful Vancouver Island in British Columbia, Canada steps away from the ocean. As much as she loves to travel, she is always so grateful to come home to her happy place on the beach.

Contact
Website: www.paddybriggs.ca

You Have Wings

By Paddy Briggs

"When she transformed into a butterfly, the caterpillars spoke not of her beauty, but of her weirdness. They wanted her to change back into what she always had been. But she had wings."

— Dean Jackson

I was 39 years old and had 3 daughters when I suddenly found myself on my own. My husband who was working in another province was living with a 26-year-old single mother with 4 young children. Suddenly, I had to be the everything – mother, father, income producer, chauffer, organizer of schedules – YES EVERYTHING! I was stunned, overwhelmed and terrified! What little bit of confidence and self-esteem I had vanished. I had always struggled with the belief that "I was not smart enough – I was not enough." I needed to make some changes in my life, and I had to do it now. The question was how?

A friend offered me a job at her office. Her employer was a Pulp & Paper Consultant and Trainer . . . he travelled all over the world with his training. My job was to photocopy and bind his training manuals. I remember thinking as I stood day after day "Is this it – is this all?"

After a particularly difficult day I came home from work, my oldest daughter was cooking dinner. I looked at my three girls and thought I can't do this anymore. I told them I wasn't feeling well and asked them to eat their dinner without me and get themselves off to bed. I walked into my room, climbed into bed with my clothes and shoes on. I slept off and on, waking up often throughout the night with the same thought – I can't do this anymore. When the alarm went off, I knew I had to get up. I felt awful. I hadn't showered, I had the same clothes on, my shoes were at the end of the bed. As I got up something happened, somewhere deep inside of me rose up. I realized YES I CAN DO THIS – I HAVE TO DO THIS – there is no one else to do it. So, get up, stop feeling sorry for yourself and figure out HOW you're going to do this!

Shortly after this experience my oldest daughter Lisa came home with a book . . . she said "Mom, I bought a book for you – I think you need it". The title was "Don't tell me it's Impossible Until After I've Already Done It by Pam Lontos." A few weeks later a friend gave me a set of tapes by Jack Canfield "Self Esteem and Peak Performance." I was now on my journey in building my confidence, my self-esteem and changing my belief about myself. I understood that if it's going to be it's up to me!

I knew I wanted to do something that would help people. A friend of my daughter's talked to me about working in a dental office. I started to do some research and it became clear that this might be a good career for me. You see, I knew I needed a career, not just a job. I found a short night school course for Dental Receptionist and enrolled. A few months later I was hired to work on the front desk of a dental office. I worked as a Dental Office Administer for 4 years. I loved working with the patients, however, I believed there was more for me – I wanted to manage a dental practice.

I continued to listen to Jack's tapes, and read other books by Napoleon Hill, Dr Denis Waitley and Les Brown. They all said the same thing; it's important to write your goals, to visualize yourself achieving that goal, to write out affirmations and repeat them every day. I learned that the more emotion and detail I included in my visualization and my affirmations the more powerful they are. What you focus your energy on is what you'll attract into your life! This is called the Law of Attraction. Jack Canfield says Ask for what you want, Believe you'll receive it, Receive what you want!

I started speaking out about what I wanted, I slowly began to believe in myself, "I am enough, I am smart, I am courageous, I am building a life for my girls and myself! My career journey had started. I started writing out my goals and affirmations, and visualizing what I wanted. Part of my journey was realizing how important it was to surround yourself with positive people, people who believed in me, people who saw something in me that I didn't see. I also realized I need to learn all I could about dentistry, I took courses, listened to tapes . . . whatever I could do to gain as much knowledge as possible about my profession.

I was asked to manage a dental clinic that was struggling, it was a perfect opportunity for me. The consultant who hired me was teaching a part time evening course for Dental Receptionist. She didn't want to teach anymore so she offered it to me. I thought – why not? As I continued to teach it, I discovered I loved teaching and training. Because of that program I got a call from the Health Sciences Continuing Studies Program Director at a local college. He asked me to meet with him regarding developing and teaching a full time Dental Receptionist Program. Me, who did not have a degree, no post-secondary education at all! I did it!

Part of the curriculum was a two-week practicum in a dental office. Through monitoring my students who were on their practicum I was asked by dentists and office managers if I did any consulting and in house training in dental offices. Their issues were generally a lack of efficient systems, and protocols or team development, communications and dealing with staff. This is how my Practice Management and Training company was developed.

Imagine that, this is all because I made a decision to change my mindset, to work on me. Becoming self-aware and deciding to change is one of the hardest things I have done . . . it is ongoing. I found that I could slip back very easily into my old way of thinking. You have to be diligent; it is an ongoing journey. One that requires support. I have to say thank you to the various transformational leaders for both their books I read and their courses that I have taken.

The one person that was a great influence on me was Jack Canfield. I had a dream of meeting him and hearing him live! One day I received a random email. Jack was coming to Seattle presenting One Day to Greatness! If you bought a ticket at that time you were allowed to bring a friend for free. I bought a ticket immediately. My daughter and I went. What an amazing life changing day! He had written a book – Success Principles and was offering an online Train the Trainer course for those of us that wanted to become a trainer in Success Principles. I enrolled and completed the training. I then went on to take further training with him which was presented partially virtual and partially live! In October of 2019 I graduated as a Transformational Coach certified by Jack Canfield. What a wonderful experience . . . who would ever have thought that I would be a part of this wonderful community of trainers. Both certifications have been incorporated into my business as a consultant and trainer in dentistry.

However, now I have a new goal; I want to coach and inspire women who have a desire to transform their lives into becoming all that they can be. To believe in themselves, to believe that they can reach their goal, to follow their dreams.

If anyone had told me years ago this is where I would be today, I would have laughed at them. Although, I always believed there was a reason I was placed on this earth. I knew in my heart of hearts there was a purpose; I just didn't know what it was. Limiting beliefs such as "I'm not enough – who am I – who would want to listen to me" always haunted me – they stopped me for years from becoming the person I wanted to be until I realized I now had wings!

I tell my story because I see so many people, especially women who don't believe in themselves, who believe they are not enough, not smart enough, that are emersed in their negative thinking. Don't let anyone or anything stop you from being all that you were meant to be – you too can transform; you too will have "wings".

Notes

Echo Layman Pelster

———— ❂ ————

❝I am in your presence as proof that no matter what happens to you, no matter what has been done to you by someone else, no matter what you have done to yourself, you can overcome the worst possible circumstances and thrive in amazing financial success, personal fulfillment and live a life of happiness and gratitude in all relationships.❞

Echo is an International Keynote Speaker, Author and Transformational Coach. She is the CEO of ENNERCOURSE, with experience of 40 years in direct sales, financial services and retail business ownership. She brings tried and true business principles and practice management tools to business organizations taking them to their next level of success. It's not about self-control, it's about self-empowerment.

Echo lives in the heart of the Sandhills of Nebraska with her husband LaVern of 25 years and their dog Cash. When she's not on the road, she enjoys writing and walking the dog.

Contact
Website: www.ennercourse.com
Email: echopelster@ennercourse.com

Releasing the Pounds of Pain

By Echo Laymon Pelster

"I turned off the noise and became comfortable in the silence of my soul, I looked for her, I listened for her, and there she was."

— Echo Laymon Pelster

I am present as proof that no matter what happens to you, no matter what someone else has done to you, no matter what you have done to yourself, you can overcome the worst possible circumstances and thrive into amazing beauty, love, and joy.

The secrets of my life and childhood were inhibiting my freedom to breathe deeply in my soul. With each tragic event, I was bound up inside myself which took me further away from who I was and my personal truth.

I spent a lot of time trying to fix my secrets, before I finally figured out that secrets couldn't be fixed, words could not be retrieved, and time is never returned to us.

I was born wanting approval. I would have given anything for my mother to want me with her and love me, but that was not my reality. She screamed, "Go find something to do, get away from me, you're a slob like your dad, I can't stand it!

My father left and my parents divorced by the time I was five. Since my parents were at war long before that, I had learned how to stay out of their way. The fighting was violent and frightful for me as a child. I was always afraid.

The only real escape for me as a child, was with my grandmother and grandfather who loved me unconditionally. They celebrated and rescued me more times than I realized as a child, and I am thankful. I think the first time I knew that food was love came from my Grandmother. I am sure she did not intend for me to get that message, but I did. When I skinned my knee it earned a cookie, if my feelings were hurt we would find a candy bar. We would talk, but we always had sweet food to comfort those real problems of childhood. I made a powerful emotional connection between food and love by 5 or 6 years old, when my parents divorced and my dad went to Vietnam.

I remember wanting to weigh 100 pounds so I would be big, and no one could hurt me anymore. This was one goal I surpassed and then some. I reached a whopping 357.8 pounds and had congestive heart failure by the time I was age 37. The doctor told me I had better do something and quick.

I felt like I didn't have much of a chance in life because of who my parents were, and I was often ashamed of them. Where you come from does affect you, your beginnings, how you think, and who you are, and I worked hard not to let that limit me.

Since I was always on my own trying to figure life out because no one wanted me around, I came to a lot of conclusions that may or may not have been accurate.

When I was nine years old my brother 'Little Joe' was hit by a train and died. I had told him I hated him that morning before I went to school and he died before I got home. I could never take those words back or say 'I'm sorry.' That conversation was one of my secrets. We saw 'Little Joe' after the accident as though we were supposed to understand death. However, we were not allowed to attend the funeral, and people brought us a lot of dessert.

I remember the lemon cake.

I remembered thinking when you die, people bring cake? What

the heck? No one told us about what happens when you die, no one explained anything. There were no comforting words, no Christian beliefs spoken or expressed, nothing. We children were left with a babysitter and people brought more cakes.

Those cakes were amazing, every bite took away the bad and sad feelings. I could eat and eat and never get full. Those desserts comforted me with every bite. I did not have to feel all the hurt and those horrible unloved feelings. I didn't realize the power of sugar then, but I recognize it and understand with great respect for myself how it works now. Unfortunately, there came a day when I couldn't eat enough to feel better. My life and moods were unpredictable, but I was aware and seeking solutions. The doctors only offered anti-depressants and diet pills, which in my mind, were not sustainable solutions.

Feelings are normal and necessary to filter though our life. As a child, I didn't know that. I was told 'Don't start balling, Suck it up, Get over it.' It's okay to laugh when it's funny, cry if you need to, and remember other people's judgment of how you look, think, believe, and feel is none of their business.

Finally, I had my first gastric bypass at 224 pounds. After the surgery, I still reached 357.8 pounds. So what did I do? I had my second gastric bypass 17 years later.

Insanity is doing the same things and expecting different results. Both times I got infections and almost died. The second time I did lose 203 pounds, made the local paper, and gained back over 100 pounds.

Ashamed and hiding out, I realized it wasn't what I was eating it was what was eating me. I got up every morning with the clear intention of "eating right and exercising" and every afternoon, me and my friend 'Little Debbie' got together again.

At first, I was excited about the next new diet and couldn't wait to get started and the next thing I know, I had failed again. I stopped telling people I was going to lose weight because I didn't believe it myself anymore.

That continued when an event happened at my Special Needs Child's school, and I was called to a parent conference to discuss the event. He was having a bad day, and I'm sure I was too. The teacher asked me how I was disciplined as a child. I told her with yelling and a belt, and I didn't want to do that to my kids. I yell a lot too. She told me there was another way called assertive discipline. I committed to give it my best.

The concept was a think for yourself and act on your own values approach. Keep your word with what you promise and follow through. Since I was not parented, I didn't know how to parent. That day I learned something new and planned to use it with my kids.

I had messed up plenty of times with my kids and myself, but after that if I told them I was going to do something for them or with them, I did. I learned that I lose my credibility with my kids when I don't keep my word. If I needed to leave some place because of poor kid behavior, we did. If the kids were good and I promised the park, we went. Things did get better in school.

I wondered if this concept would work to lose weight?

I had been on every diet or close to every diet that was ever published. I had white knuckled it though plenty of family dinners, only to feel deprived and stressed by family to go home and make a cake and eat the whole thing myself. After eating the cake, the guilt alone was unbearable, but I wondered would a concept program work?

Not an "eat this food or don't eat that food," but something that I could tie to my own values.

It was a day-by-day process, where I had to consciously decide, eat the fish and spit out the bones in my life. I had to start cleaning up my life, my past, my relationships, my decisions, and my indecision. I started reading books, at first it was diet magazines, but people do not fail at dieting, diets fail people. I had decisions to make and things to decide.

One of the biggest discoveries I made was just because it comes packaged as food, does not mean that it contains true, authentic food. I had to decide if an ingredient I could not pronounce was something I was truly willing to put into my body.

I discovered I was addicted to sugar. Sugar is 30 times more addictive than heroin. It is in everything! I took 100% responsibility for my awareness.

It took 5 days for my stomach to growl when I started to eat out of hunger instead of emotion, it was wonderful! I waited one more hour to make sure, I wasn't driven by my habits, fears, or cravings. When sugar cravings are fed, they get bigger. If you starve them, they go away.

I came through some messy circumstances, including the tragic deaths and burials of four siblings, a special needs child, being raped, two broken marriages, bankruptcy, put into foster care by my mother at age 15, but those events are not my identity or my value. (My mother is still living and refuses to see me. I no longer hear her voice, and I choose to give her grace.)

I am my own person today. I am not owned by anyone or anything. I am a beautiful, sensitive, loving, capable, intelligent businesswoman who finds joy in helping others transform their lives on their terms with their values. I am a woman who keeps her agreements with herself and others.

Every event that I went through was a learning experience. It may not have been perfect, and yet it helped form the amazing women that I am today.

I am perfect, and so are you. I couldn't be here without all those crooked paths first, and the journeys of life are sometimes hard and treacherous, but the satisfaction of staying the course has been rewarding and blessed.

The answers were not in what I ate or didn't eat, they were inside me. The place that was hardest to go had the most reward. Realizing that secrets couldn't be fixed, only unveiled, and revealed, I examined the stories I told myself. I rethought my thoughts, and I found humor in how naïve I was and still am.

I found gratitude in everyday actions that were in alignment with my goal to be a normal weight. I read somewhere normal is a setting on a dryer, and I am not a dryer.

Even if you have not received humanity from the previous generation, what you've learned will be passed on from you.

I chose to turn off the noise and become comfortable in the quiet of my soul. I looked for myself, listened for me, and there I was. A super special, unique, exquisite, eccentric, happy, fun, humorous, empathetic, kind, loving, helpful, transformational coach, and keynote speaker.

Release yourself from the noise, listen closely, hear your heart, feel you calling quietly and there you will be.

Release yourself from the noise, listen closely to hear your heart, and feel your true self quietly calling. There you will be. ✤

Notes

Jennie Ritchie

Jennie Ritchie is a Certified Canfield Trainer in the Success Principles and a Certified Life Coach. After teaching middle and high school for 25 years and authoring the Amazon best-selling book: "Keeping it Together When Life Throws You Curves" she began her second career as a speaker and coach.

Jennie is passionate about helping others create their best life and is an expert in translating personal development principles into real-world language. In addition to writing chapters in many best-selling collaborative books, she and her mom are soon to release a book on the topic of Reinvention. No matter where you are, or where you've been, Jennie can help you believe in yourself and remember that anything is possible.

In addition to coaching, Jennie enjoys her full-time work managing a coach community. Jennie resides in Southern California with her husband of 34 years, Wally, and their mini husky.

Contact

Website: www.jennieritchie.com

Becoming Calmer

By Jennie Ritchie

"The greater the level of calmness of our mind, the greater our peace of mind, the greater our ability to enjoy a happy and joyful life"

— Dalai Lama

My life has always felt crazy. I am the queen of overthinking, overdoing, taking care of everyone else and running as soon as my feet hit the floor in the morning. I have been a slave to my 'to-do' list for most of my adult life. Of course, there were vacations, life before children, and other relaxing times, but I have often lived my life running around like a chicken with little emphasis on self-care! I know many of you can relate.

In the past, I made commitments to myself to meditate, take deep breaths and prioritize self-care, but my efforts were short-lived.

When we moved from Utah back to Orange County, California in 2019, I gave up my teaching career to build my own coaching and speaking business. Living by the beach was cool, but try as I might, I wasn't making the time to get there as often as I wanted. In addition to building my business, I was working a part-time job. After March of 2020, our youngest child, a high school junior, began suffering from anxiety, which was a new and concerning situation. Not to mention the financial stress from the increased cost-of-living. There were positives about living in Southern California again, like being closer to family and the great weather. In some ways, life was less crazy, but in many ways, it was more.

Last year, I was approached by a doctor who needed help organizing, editing and printing her book on hormone balance. I agreed to take half the payment in trade for my own hormone testing and consultation. As part of the testing, I collected my saliva four times in a 24-hour period and sent it to the lab for analysis. When the results came back, they showed elevated cortisol levels in all four samplings. Basically, according to my body, I was living each day in a constant 'fight or flight' state. I often felt some level of stress, but this was my body confirming that I was stressed throughout the day.

A second experience confirmed what my body was trying to tell me. I have a habit of frequently clearing my throat . . . it's a bothersome habit for me and annoys those around me. I visited an Ear, Nose & Throat doctor who tried to isolate the problem. He said, "It might be post-nasal drip, reflux or something entirely different." After a few tests, he recommended I consult a gastroenterologist and perhaps have an endoscopy. I got on a video visit with a gastro doctor and after talking to him for less than 15 minutes, he said, "I don't think it's merely post-nasal drip . . . I think it's also related to stress and anxiety." My reaction was, "What?!?!"

Later that night, we went out to dinner with friends, and I told them about the doctor's video visit prognosis. The husband said, "What do you have to be stressed about?"

That really got me thinking. What did I have to be stressed about? Some stress is normal for everyone, but I started to see that much of my stress was caused by my own thinking, my mental habits and my familiar way of handling life.

When we come upon a transformation in life, it is usually accompanied by new eyes to see and new awarenesses.

I started by getting honest with myself . . . really honest . . . examining two of my core beliefs.

First, early in life I adopted the idea that I needed to take care of situations and people around me. When I was young, our family consisted of me, my mom and my younger sister. As time went on, I formed the belief that it was my job to take care of them. This belief has driven me to try and take care of everyone and everything in my sphere.

Over time, I've become aware of this belief and I can now see the ways it has affected me as an adult. One way is in my lack of boundaries and people-pleasing tendencies. I've often said 'yes' when I wanted to say 'no'. Another is in prioritizing others above myself . . . even when they didn't need me!

Another belief I developed was the desire for credit and praise from others. In high school I got a lot of 'gold stars' from my teachers and others around me. I was involved in plenty of activities, did well academically and received consistent praise. I liked it. I can see now that I began to seek praise and credit, looking to others for value and validation. This eventually led to the idea that, "If I'm productive I'm worthy", which in turn led to perfectionism, overthinking and setting unrealistic expectations for myself.

A good person doesn't screw up the colonoscopy prep instructions. A good person recycles. Who made these decisions? High expectations have often led me to overschedule or hold on too tight to a certain outcome, only to watch the balls drop . . . painting myself as the victim.

This search for outside praise also created unhealthy habits of comparison and judgement (of myself and others).

Here's another example: Whenever we have a family event or project, like leaving for a trip or having a dinner party, I usually end up stressed out, which then stresses everyone around me.

In these times, I'd look around and ask myself, "Why do I have to do everything? Why isn't anyone pitching in". Looking back, it's often because I was doing more than I needed to do or they knew they wouldn't be able to do it like I wanted it done . . . so better for them not to pitch in at all. It wasn't a good system for maintaining healthy relationships. However, it didn't have to be this way. We were going to get from Point A to Point B anyway . . . Could the journey be more enjoyable?

Another habit that caused stress in my life was not being present. When I was busy working on one task, be it the dishes or typing a document, my mind often veered unconsciously to thinking about other things I should have been doing or that needed to get done. This was a very stressful way to live . . . and I'd been doing it most of my life.

In November 2021, I started to see things more clearly. I knew I didn't want to be that person forever. I was ready to make some changes in order to live a calmer, less stressed life. I decided that my word for 2022 was going to be "Calm".

However, you know as well as I do that real transformation takes more than a word.

It takes an initial decision and an ongoing commitment; not to mention the awareness to 'catch' yourself when you're slipping into old habits and reset.

I had to question the belief that I need to take care of everyone else. Do I really need to do that? No. They are or will be fine. It is OK to take care of myself . . . and even before caring for others sometimes. Realizing that they can do their thing and I can do mine is both freeing and stress relieving.

I'm reinforcing the new belief that my physical, mental and emotional health matter, which involves putting my needs first. It's a different feeling for me . . . a good feeling. I'm learning that time spent on myself is not wasted. It's easier now that my children are grown. Being a working mom with three young children made it difficult to squeeze in self-care. But I believe that no matter what stage of life we're in, we can make time (even a bit) to take care of ourselves.

I've also realized that I don't need to get all the gold stars. It's OK to lower my expectations for myself or not do everything perfectly.

One day, my husband and I took separate cars up to Los Angeles for a funeral. On the way home, I had planned to go to our storage unit to drop off some items from our move. It was nearly 8 pm and I was in a dress and heels. I was playing the martyr role as I thought to myself, "Poor me. I have to go storage. No one else has to go to storage." It was then I realized that I had a choice; I could choose not to go. I realized that the junk could stay in the trunk for another few days. I went home and it felt great. I wasn't a victim and that was progress for me!

Learning to say 'no' when someone asks me to do something I would rather not is still tough. However, I am reinforcing the idea that I don't have to please everyone.

My other epiphany is that maybe, just maybe . . . I don't have to change the world. My goal: to sit on the couch and watch a show with my husband without feeling compelled to multitask or guilty because I'm relaxing. The idea that I'm not doing enough . . . that I need to do more is fading.

Besides questioning my beliefs and changing my mental and physical habits, I am employing other calming tactics . . .

1. **Trusting.** Trust is having faith that everything is going to work out . . . and I don't have to figure it all out. It's knowing that everything is going to be fine – that it'll get figured out somehow. For me, calmness comes with trusting and goes hand in hand with gratitude (the secret sauce for lowering stress).

2. **Identify Elements of Joy.** I love the calming effect of the sunset, riding my bike, listening to music and taking a full deep breath. I also love the soothing influence of essential oils, being in nature. Laughter brings me joy, so I'm working on doing it more.

3. **Giving myself grace.** We often extend grace to others without giving it to ourselves. I am learning to give myself the permissions I normally only give others – to let go of some things, to rest, to forgive myself and lower my expectations.

4. **Follow the Leader.** There are some women in my life who naturally have a calm vibe. I watch to see how they handle a dinner party and follow their example. You know the ones . . . those who remain calm when things are chaotic. In the past, I might have judged her and thought . . . how can she be calm? But now I am ready to embrace change.

How am I becoming a calmer person? By getting intentional and being present. By deciding what's important to me and protecting it. By being willing to let some things go and forgiving myself in the same breath.

Just so we're clear . . . I have not mastered this process yet. I'm still learning. I've spent my whole life forming these habits and they don't flip in a day. I truly believe that if you want to make a change in your life, start with a baby step. Even though we want to change everything at once, that rarely works. Create one new habit, one new replacement thought, one different way of responding and stick to it. Then, set realistic expectations and be patient with yourself.

What change do you want to make? If I can do it, you can do it. Let's create transformation together. ✿

Notes

Our Invitation to You

We honor you for investing in yourself by reading, receiving and feeling our love and support through our stories of grit and determination.

We hope you feel connected and share in our intention to make a difference in the world with our words of inspiration.

Create a safe space to transform in your life, your community and your world. Tell us about it on our facebook page: www.facebook.com/thebookontransformation.

Ask questions or request information on writing a chapter in one of our upcoming Inspired Life Series books: The Book on Gratitude and The Book on Abundance.

Attend a virtual or live Transformation or Writer Retreat, or inspire others with pure Transformation Essential Oil . . . reach out to us at info@thebookontransformation.com.

Stay in touch with our Inspired Team at
www.thebookontransformation.com

We are "Transforming the World Together."

Love,

Jan

Made in the USA
Middletown, DE
15 January 2023

21743623R00136